MEASURE
of the
YEAR

MEASURE
of the
YEAR

By Roderick L. Haig-Brown

Essay Index Reprint Series

BOOKS FOR LIBRARIES PRESS
FREEPORT, NEW YORK

INTERNATIONAL STANDARD BOOK NUMBER:
0-8369-2191-7

LIBRARY OF CONGRESS CATALOG CARD NUMBER:
79-142637

PRINTED IN THE UNITED STATES OF AMERICA

CONTENTS

v

Contents

FOREWORD

I HAVE WRITTEN HERE OF MY family almost without meaning to, but that is natural enough since marriage and family are immeasurably the most important things that can happen to any man. I say I have written of them. Rather, they have come into the book inevitably, taken it over and in large measure made it. Ann is my wife, with whom I have now lived through sixteen years of steadily growing understanding and unity. Valerie is my eldest child, one day less than fourteen at this writing. Mary Charlotte is two years her junior. Alan is my son, baptized on Pearl Harbor Sunday and named for his grandfather who died in the first war. Celia is our post-war daughter, not yet three. Uncle Reg is our neighbor, now seventy, British Columbia born, pioneer and man of honor, close friend of many years.

It was necessary to list this cast of characters because, as I say, they have come into the book with a casual inevitability that caught me unawares and let them by without any other close identification.

If a book must have a clear purpose beyond mere sharing

of experience, the purpose of this book is to show a family trying to live out a sensible and positive life in the twentieth century, trying to keep on terms with its world and yet not be too much fooled by it. I have tried to describe the concrete factors that surround the life of this particular family and the more abstract issues that affect it. This family lives in the country, so things of the country have a heavy emphasis. But it does so in a civilization that is primarily urban, with remarkably good communications, so it escapes few of the things that affect all families. It may set up slightly different defenses against some of them, and so doing may be part of the reason for living in the country. But it cannot escape them and does not want to escape them, only to meet them on its own terms and solve them.

I have left out many important things—religion, for instance, and music. The first of these must be implicit throughout the book, in every approach to everything shown, or else I misunderstand the meaning and value of religion. The second is more typical of the many important things I have left out; though I am fond of music and often deeply stirred by it, I do not trust my knowledge or understanding far enough to write about it. If Ann were writing the book she undoubtedly would put it in, as she would put many other things differently or with different emphasis.

While this way of living is my main theme, at least one minor theme follows through with it all the way: that is the account of natural life and changing seasons carried by the "month" chapters, a thread that strengthens and supports and gives depth to the other. Such variations as the magistrate chapters are both on the theme and from the theme. The theme in which they are set gives them increased meaning, while their own inherent values give body to the theme. To put that concretely, a man's performance on the bench is undoubtedly affected by the type and quality of his life at home; the fact that a man is a professional writer, a hunter, a fisherman, a magistrate, undoubtedly has influence on almost every phase of his family's life.

I have written about some things that it is difficult to touch on at all without seeming pretentious or smug or both—unless one evades the issue by being trivial. I have done so in all humility and with all the honesty I can find in myself; if my measures of humility and honesty are too light to carry the load, this is a chance I have to take, because I believe it is important for ordinary men as well as great men to state themselves.

It seems of some importance that we are Canadians. Not that by this our problems are greatly different from those of most American families, but that our approaches may be. We live by a slightly different machinery of government, another variant of the active creation that is western democracy. We are not citizens of a giant power that can shape the world or shake it by physical force alone. Nor do we look forward to becoming such a power. We are a strong and active minor power that is still growing, and growing rather fast, with a long way to go. Of all the minor powers we are closest to and most like the United States. Yet we are different, we expect to grow differently and to remain different. We believe that in this natural independence of thought and being in small powers is the only hope of effective world government; so it is well that the great powers should know something of us and of what we think.

Again, this has meaning only against the frame of living, down on the level of ordinary people breathing and talking and eating and sleeping and trying to be themselves. Living, for any family, is enormous diversity. Only a fraction of the diversity that makes our own living is in this book, but this fraction is meant to be enough to bring us alive, to make us ordinary people.

All this is the solemn purpose of my book, the only apology I can make for it. The rest is pleasure and gratitude, with no more serious intent than to share experience with other people in the hope that they will enjoy it by recognizing patterns of their own pleasures or reflections of their own gratitude. When all is said and done, a writer can have no more serious purpose than this. His duty is to stir echoes in his readers, to touch thought and ideas that might otherwise have remained idle and forgotten in the back of the mind. It is a rare book that changes a life; a poor one that adds nothing to it. I have tried to add by showing our own confusions and prides, our pleasures and worries and attempts to grow.

R. H-B.

Campbell River, B. C.
24th April, 1950.

MEASURE
of the
YEAR

MARCH

Spring on the pacific coast of Canada is not normally reluctant. In a good year there should be at least a few seeds planted in the vegetable garden by March 15. This year March 15 went by and the garden was not even plowed. There was snow on the ground from December 1 until the last days of the month; there is still snow under the alders behind the barn and under the shadow of the river bank, and there is still frost in the ground, as I found when I tried to move some trees last week.

The first ten days of March were beautiful, warm, and full of sunlight, with only light breezes. On March 8 a swarm of robins passed through. I heard them first, as I came back from milking in the morning, then saw them all over the lawn and through the main orchard. During the day I went up the river and when I came home towards evening there were more robins than ever, through the Big Fir pasture, in the willows and small alders along the river bank below the vegetable garden; at least a hundred of them, the breasts of the males warmly and brilliantly red in the evening sun, their voices lively, their wings flashingly active. It seemed like spring to see them there and the day felt like spring, yet there was still the pale brown of the pastures, the feeling of ice under the thawed surface of the ground, the hint of a night's frost to come on the evening air.

Nearly a week later I went up the river again. It was raining and the rain changed to sleet, then snow. It was bitterly cold, far colder than the coldest day of winter, with a sodden power to drain away warmth from any exposed part of the body. Such days and such cold belong peculiarly to the months between the seasons, to November before winter is fully come, to March before spring warmth has worked its way into the ground.

Spring has come when the earth is warm to the hands that work it. There was no such warmth in the March soil this year, and it was clear by the middle of the month that there would not be. But it is the countryman's concern to take fullest advantage of spring's coming by anticipating it, so he watches for signs to guide him—gropingly, hopefully, with the measure of faith that his nature permits him. Some things were as usual this year. The mallard greenheads came to the river and the mergansers paired in their time. By mid-February the black sea brant were moving into the Gulf of Georgia on their northward migration. The mass of robins was a few days late; March 2 or 3 is more usual here in this little block of twenty acres on which we live. Frogs should be croaking on the east side of the house by the second week of the month; that week passed and the next, and I had not heard them. There was no green in the tops of the alders, no generous swell of leaf bud in willow or ground maple or salmonberry. In an early year the maple seedlings show their first narrow, flat leaves at the very beginning of the month;

as the month ended the hard shells began to crack and the roots to thrust down.

Perhaps there is not much sense in watching for signs, in saying over and over, "This is a late spring," or "Looks like an early year." But to watch the signs and say these things is a rite among men and it has meaning; strongest meaning for those who are closest to the soil and the weather, but strong meaning for all men, even those who live most determinedly in the cities and shield themselves most closely from the rigors of winter and the caprices of spring. Even today, in the most modern of cities, man has not been able to make himself altogether independent of the weather, and perhaps that is a good thing.

The great clear signs of the changing seasons, the migrations of geese and salmon, of caribou and buffalo, the swell of leaf buds in spring, the first fall snow on the high mountains, have meaning beyond themselves and a power of association that must go far back into the earliest development of man. They have passed, many of them, through wonder into superstition and religion, and are now become wonder again and living pleasure. One observes them because they are inescapable and responds to them in the sanction of long usage. But for every one of these there are a thousand lesser signs, persistent in their multiplying variation from year's end to year's end and through all the seasons. Some are signs of changing season, some of progressing seasons, some of nothing more than their own change and growth. There is little concrete reason to watch them, yet men have always watched them, often with intense pleasure, and many men have thought it worthwhile to record them minutely and faithfully.

Observation of this kind holds its own satisfactions and lively triumphs; it is full of surprises and rediscoveries, of new sensations and sensations renewed. By themselves these would

be enough. But over and above them all is the sense of participation in the world's real life, of steadily increasing intimacy,
of possession that grows gradually stronger over the years.

It may seem strange to write of observation as participation,
but no man is solely an observer of the natural world, the
countryman least of all. We are all basically hunters or gardeners, gleaners or predators, we all feel the weather on our
faces at times, and the things that stir and change about us
stir within us also.

So this year spring is late. But now, at the end of the month,
the things of spring have come. Crocuses are in bloom, daffo-
dils in bud, the frogs are croaking on both sides of the house,
the snow is gone from under the shadow of the hill. There
were two nights without frost and moths came to the lighted
windowpane; behind them, seen only occasionally through the
darkness, a bat wheeled and hunted. Stone flies and the big
orange crane flies hatched out and blundered up from the
river. One morning, almost at the end of the month, swallows
were flying back and forth over the ridge on the far side of
the river, then they were down along the river itself and out
over the fields. The scarlet shoots of the peonies are bright in
the border and the leaf buds of the horse chestnuts have burst
out of their shiny covers. The sheep are finding grass in the
pastures as only sheep can, and the cowbirds strut there and
the robins bob and lean their heads to listen for worms.

There have been other things during the month. The vivid
laugh of the great pileated woodpeckers, the mating flights
of the ravens, slow, intricate repetitions, marked by the liquid,
urgent voices of the competing males. There have been the
paired mergansers in every eddy of the river, the coppery
shower of catkins on the alders, the first show of dogtooth
violets and false Solomon's-seal along the banks of the river.
Seen or unseen, heard or unheard, these things must happen

here in March. I hope for them and turn quickly to the first warning, but I do not watch for them. There is an important difference. One is play, the other is work.

Both yield records: the first a casual record of pleasure in the memory, the second a written record of dates and times and places that is likely to be important. The first is a gentle art, yet a part of living; the second is positive science.

How far I am from science I know from the experience of the purple finches. For many years I saw them first in the flowers of the big maple by the back door and happily considered them returning spring migrants. Then, five or six years ago, I saw a pair in mid-January as I crossed the old orchard, to the east of the house. I thought it unusual, noted carefully that I could see only grey in the female, without the overlay of green one notices later—then forgot all about it and went back to expecting purple finches with the maple flowers. Last winter, just after Christmas, Ann and I went down to Tom Hudson's farm at the mouth of the river to skate. The trees around the house were full of purple finches. "They're always here," Tom said. "And they eat all the buds off the cherry trees." A week later I saw two pairs at my neighbor's house. And a week later than that a male was feeding with the towhees and juncos at my own house.

So much for the precision and scientific value of my own observations. In fifteen years I have learned that purple finches winter comfortably here on the Pacific Coast, just north of the fiftieth parallel. I shall still welcome their migrant brothers and sisters when they come, two or three weeks from now, to hang on the maple flowers, brighter blossom than the tree will bear of its own sap run.

PROPER NAMES

W HEN A FAMILY HAS LIVED IN one place for several years it becomes a place of many names. This of necessity, as the family goes about its daily affairs; the names grow out of efforts at description for the most part —it is not easy to assign them. The children think up many names and discard most of them in time. Only the other day Ann asked, "Where's Alan?"

"He was playing in Kingdom Come a few minutes ago," Mary said.

"Kingdom Come?"

"Don't you know where that is? Out there, the hollow in the big field where we broke the ice last winter."

"Who calls it that?"

"Joey said he was going to hit a ball to Kingdom Come the other day, and that's how far it went. So we all call it that now."

So there is a new place name, overly pretentious perhaps for a rolling dip four or five feet deep and only a hundred feet or so across, but useful and therefore likely to last.

The land we live on is a rough square of twenty acres, based on eight or nine hundred feet of river bank. The river is the Elk, four hundred feet wide at this point, swift and broken, flowing from west to east. A dusty gravel road divides the twenty acres, nine acres on the river side of the road, eleven acres on the other side. The house stands just about in the center of the nine acres on the river side, rather over a hundred feet from the edge of the river.

March

The barn is on the far side of the road and three or four acres of rough clearing around it make up the Barn Field. Behind that are the Alders, a swampy thicket of alder and maple and salmonberry with a pleasant creek flowing through one corner—Kingfisher Brook, as a matter of fact, though I have never heard the name used and know it only from an old plan I once saw in a real-estate office. On that side of the road a missing person or thing can only be in one of three places —"over at the barn" which would include a check on the chicken house forty or fifty feet away; "in the Barn Field"; or "back in the Alders."

This side of the road is much more complicated, chiefly because it has been fenced into small enclosures which pasture ten or fifteen black sheep. East of the house there is a one-acre pasture along the road: Richardson's Field to the children. Between that and the river is the Old Orchard, a collection of plum and cherry and pear trees of which only a Bartlett pear and two yellow egg-plums are really useful trees. Then there is the Hedge, a hundred-and-fifty-foot line of Douglas firs, moved in from the woods ten or twelve years ago and clipped each summer. Inside that is the Border, a twelve-foot strip of perennials, then the Lawn.

The Study juts out into the Lawn from the rest of the house. From under the study window the Rose Border runs down to the river, dividing the lawn from the Main Orchard —eight mature apple trees, a prolific Italian prune, and two quinces.

Between the house and the road is the Driveway and the Birches, a strip of rough ground where two thick, dark green balsams dominate twenty or thirty birch trees and other hardwoods I have planted over the years. West of the house are the Garage and the Cottage, backed by a stand of tall evergreens. West of these again are two more fields, the Poplar

Field (wherein lies Kingdom Come) and the Big Fir Field. Along the river, from the edge of the Main Orchard well out into the Big Fir Field, is the Vegetable Garden.

All that, of course, is just an outline of proper names. There should be far more names and far more capitals to do the thing justice. There is the River Bank, for instance, and along it all manner of identifications. Uncle Reg's Water Wheel, just downstream of the easterly line fence. The Balm of Gilead Tree, tall and splendidly shaped with roots swarming down the eroded bank like oversize pythons. Near these roots is the Secret Place, a tiny cave under the base of a willow tree which the children found a year or two ago and whose entrance they marked with stone-edged paths and flowers in Mason jars.

The strip of bank below the cribbing at the foot of the lawn is too open to have served many purposes or to need close identification. But just above it is the lower end of the Swimming Place, behind the Dam. Until I changed it a few years ago this was a series of three or four canoe bays, built by Indians who piled rocks across the current to form narrow stalls in which they could beach their canoes. We simply extended this idea by piling all the rocks into a wing dam, using a horse and blocks to move the largest ones. The wing dam breaks the current effectively enough at most summer levels and the removal of the rocks has left a fair depth of water below the dam.

Beside the Swimming Place are the Terraces, the lower only a couple of feet above low water and held by a rock retaining wall, the higher shaded by a thick balsam tree and well above anything except the river's fullest freshet.

The canoe bays carried on above the dam and it was a simple matter to put two into one and make the Canoe Landing, a place where I can swing the big Peterborough canoe into moderate shelter from either up- or downstream approach. It is satisfying to continue the old use and my canvas-covered freighter is a worthy successor to the finest of the high-prowed dugouts.

Above the Canoe Landing, under the vegetable garden fence, alders and willows are thick along the river bank and trilliums and dogtooth violets grow in profusion clear up to Alan's Cabin, on the Line Fence Pool. Alan's Cabin is Alan's work, his care, and deep concern. I help on it occasionally under his instructions, but the walls of old fence posts have been going up slowly for over two years now and we may not get the roof on it until towards the end of this summer. In its first stages it seemed to me an unpromising structure, fated to early collapse and never likely to seem handsome. The sand floor slopes riverwards and the walls slope the same way, in spite of our attempts to straighten them. The fence posts are of odd sizes and the rotten ends that were once underground leave awkward spaces in the walls. Yet it will be shelter when it is finished and it will be Alan's own. And I have learned to love the way it fits in among the trees. Several times last winter it welcomed me as I came up out of the heavy water of the Line Fence Pool with a freshly gaffed steelhead. Sitting on one of the half-built walls to fill a pipe and let the cold draw out of me into the air I felt the qualities of hearth and home, as I imagine Alan feels them, in the man-made place. The hot rum waiting up at the house seemed a less urgent matter than it had a few moments before.

These are the big names, the important ones that we all use often. There are many others, and many, I'm sure, of which Ann and I know nothing; there are even some that the children themselves have used for a while and forgotten. I suppose that is the eventual fate of all such highly local and intimate place names; they serve their brief purpose and die as the children grow up or the places change. It must have happened clear across the continent from Atlantic to Pacific and all through the Old World as well. Under St. Paul's Cathedral and Westminster Hall, in the foundations of the Bastille, beneath the Vatican, the Colosseum, the Acropolis, must be the place names of generations of country children. In North America the generations may have been fewer, but the names would have been no less intensely lived and used until the sidewalks of the great cities came to bury them without a trace. Yet I like to think that one here or there, especially apt or simply persistent, may have outlasted all the changes, naming concrete or asphalt where it once named loam or gravel or swamp or creek.

The children's names go beyond the narrow limits of the line fences now, but once beyond these they have lesser urgency and even briefer life; the names of the real world exist out there and can be referred to accurately enough for most purposes—the railroad tracks, the slough, the Power Commission, the Construction Camp, over across the river, down at the beach, and so on. They do what is needed and most will surely outlive the closer names. But for the change of seasons and the feel of living in it, I like to think of the outside world apart from these names. There is the Salt-water, through Discovery Passage, among the islands, across the breadth of the Gulf of Georgia; and beyond that, the Mainland Mountains. Towards home again the Tidal River, then the Cleared Land—our own and a few other farms on the flat immediately above tidewater. Beyond that again the Alder Thickets and the Stream Bottoms, the Open Logging Works and the First Lakes, then the Deep Woods and more lakes, and the High Mountains of the heart of Vancouver Island beyond them all. The seasons and the year's brief times are lived differently through each of these levels, and the vague names

I have set down here in capitals are less names than simplified physical geography.

Because one knows the different levels it is possible to live each season half a dozen times. The snow will disappear from the edge of the salt-water a full week before it is gone here at the house. When it is gone from here it will still be lying among the alders, rotten and twig-scarred, the old snow of a finished winter but still snow. For a month after that it will be deep around the far lakes and perhaps fresh snow will fall there. On the high mountains it is still twenty feet deep and will last beyond midsummer; I have seen August snow only a thousand feet above sea level, in a slide on the northern face of a mountain.

It is the same with almost everything that happens. The hummingbirds work the salmonberry blossoms here in April and May—back at the far lakes you will find them doing the same thing in July. Tiger lilies bloom along the lower river in late May and early June—you may find them again in the deep woods along the beds of the little streams in fullest August heat.

Or there is the other way of using the seasons at their different levels. The ducks and geese migrate along the seaway, seldom coming over the house. Yet they do at times pass over; a flock of Canadas towards a stormy dusk, seeking a place to rest through the night; or the high, multiple wedge of snow geese that Valerie and I watched one day as they swung and their wings caught the sunlight.

"Like strings of electric lights," she said.

"No," I said. "Not that."

"Well then, like dewdrops on spiderwebs in the early morning." And I knew she was right.

Always enough of this to remind one of the great movement passing through just beyond sight, barely a mile or two away. Having seen once, the mind remembers and sees again, because it is the time of year. Remembers and sees the snow melting back from the rocky slopes of the mountains and saxifrage blooming almost in the moment that the white edge draws away. Remembers the dwarf dogwood's massed immaculate flowers on the mossy log beside the spring at the edge of the trail, and feels their clear and perfect whiteness in that month of every year. Remembers the movement of the blue grouse back to the timber in the first stormy weather of October, transforms the icy rain sweeping before a November gale into the driven, needle-sharp snow particles of six thousand feet above sea level. And in these rememberings each day of the year and its happenings is multiplied, each season finds new dimensions of depth and meaning.

Along with the children's temporary names and the permanent ones of nature, there are those of day-to-day living. Four or five hundred yards downstream, the Highway Bridge. Half a mile down the road, the Store and the Meat Market. One mile beyond these, the School; until a year or two ago the children walked there or rode their bicycles and were, I think, the better for it. Half a mile beyond that again the Wharf, the Post Office and the cluster of more imposing stores that now with the Firehall, the Bank, the Movie Theater, and a few garages make up the center of the village. Everything beyond the School seems distant. One may go down that way once or twice a week, but it is still distant, only close when one is coming home to it from Vancouver or Victoria or Seattle. A few years ago the Post Office was important, but now that a rural mail route passes the front gate it is only indirectly so; one knows that it handles mail, but does not feel dependence.

All this lies east and south, down the highway, down the

Island. Ten years ago our nearest neighbor across the river, to the north, was a full mile away. To the west there was nothing nearer than seven miles—the Lodge at the lower lake. Now we have four neighbors within the first mile, then the Power House with its eight or ten houses, the forest nursery where Bracken Prairie used to be, and the Construction Camp up by the first dam. In a little while the Camp will disappear, the rest will remain, the Lodge moved sixty or seventy feet up the hill to be above the reach of the lake's new level.

Except for the logging and the dam-building it is gradual change, and even these swift, gigantic changes settle back into gradualness—the restoration of soil and the slow regrowth of trees in the logging slash; the slow weathering down of the new lakes behind the dams, and of the dams themselves. Our own change has been slow too, and continues slow. Thirty years ago these acres were logging slash and stumps along the river bank. Twenty-seven years ago this frame house was new and the great maple at the southwest corner was little more than a sapling. We are second settlers, still stump ranchers. Over the years we have lived in it we've changed the house and added on to it. Ten years ago we seeded the lawn, made the border, and cribbed the vulnerable parts of the river bank. Probably we shall go on changing things, planting more trees, putting up new fences, taming raw spots to special uses. But without urgency, I hope, so that in twenty or thirty years' time the children's place names will have the use and meaning they have today.

CANADA

CANADA IS A LARGE MODERN
country with a small population. I don't know any way of saying that dramatically enough to express its full meaning. It means that something less than fifteen million people are the tenants of three and a half million square miles; most of them are concentrated in or near a dozen big cities dotted along a three-thousand-mile southern border. Wilderness marches almost from the back door of the city slum. Modern factory, modern airfield, modern office building are dusted with the ash of the pioneer's clearing fires. Any Canadian can look outward almost to infinity, and call it all his own.

Canada has been developed within an empire, under the shadow of an enormously powerful and populous neighbor, by immigrants from every race and nation on the face of the earth. All her geographical boundaries run north and south, across the face of the country instead of along her borders. She has two languages, ten sharply separate provinces, and many religions. There has been, again and again, bitter misunderstanding, friction approaching violence, between French and English—or between Canadians and *les Canadiens* as Hugh MacLennan puts it. Yet Canada is a nation, with a sure and solid unity, a working faith in her own entity and integrity that has completely transcended all these practical difficulties.

It is fashionable to deny this, to say that Canadians are provincial, or British, or American. For my money it is a stupid and tiresome fashion, born out of ignorance and literal-mindedness and the wretched inferiority of inferior people. One had only to be in England during the war to know that Canadians were neither British nor American in the narrow sense of both words. And, being Canadian, one not only knew it but felt it, which is the true test. Canadians walked differently, behaved differently, and looked different, even when wearing the British battledress that so many nationalities wore in those times.

It is not that a Canadian feels alien in Britain—he feels rather a sense of partnership, almost of common ownership, yet always with the reservation that he is himself and his own. A Canadian in the United States has much the same feeling; his sense of partnership is economic, industrial, and geographic, rather than institutional and traditional. Yet Americans and Canadians share some traditions that British and Canadians do not: traditions of mass immigration and western movement, of the opening up of land and the development of a country without hereditary rulers.

To some extent this may be a western view rather than an eastern. The east has many descendants of the United Empire Loyalists and they are not always willing to admit a close heritage with the United States. Yet even in the east there is ready and constant interchange across the border and nearly every Canadian seems to have relations to the south.

Which brings me squarely against the charge that Canadians are provincial. Of course they are. What does the cockney know of rural England, or the countryman of London? What does the New Yorker know of the Pacific Coast, or the Middle Westerner of either? Canadians are divided by enormous distances, by the Laurentians, by the great Canadian shield, by the Rockies, by the Coast Range. They are divided by language and by the inherited misunderstandings of the years —not too long ago—when travel was infinitely slower and more difficult than it is today. They have made themselves into a nation in spite of these things, against the logic of mountains and language and distance. If in doing so they have not immediately overcome that logic, surely it is no great cause for wonder and despair. Rather it is proof that the difficulties were real and that unity in spite of them called for more solid faith and stronger courage than most young nations possess.

I'm not at all sure that provincialism is such an evil thing at that. No man becomes a great patriot without first learning the closer loyalties and learning them well: loyalty to the family, to the place he calls home, to his province or state or county; and I'm sure as I am of Canada that no man will ever give real service to a world state without first being a true patriot. Nor do I think that provincialism will die or even greatly lessen in Canada. Here on the Pacific Coast we shall always feel the pull of the great American coast cities, of Seattle, Portland, San Francisco, Los Angeles, just as surely as the Maritimer will tend to New England, Montreal and Toronto will know New York, and our prairie people will know their brothers of the American plains. But Canadian law is over all of us, a Canadian way of thought is ours. We shall hold them and build on them because we believe they have meaning and worth.

Make no mistake, though. This sense of unity across the American border is no small and feeble thing. It is real and living, a bond between people, a continuation of known and beloved country, and it is part of being Canadian. When I am south on Puget Sound I feel a pride of ownership and partnership not unlike that I feel when I see Westminster Hall or Winchester Cathedral or Wordsworth's Lake District or Hardy's Dorset. It is a pride of belonging, of knowing that the people who live among these waterways and forests and mountains will have an understanding and warmth for me, as I have for them. It is not difficult for a Canadian to feel foreign in the United States, especially in the cities. There is the chromium-plated bigness, the large, outgoing, prideful American character that Americans have built for each other, the change of pace, in giving and getting, buying and selling, living and dying. But these things are absorbed in a day or so, to be revived only in the intensity of friendship that grows from the chance discovery by a shoeshine boy, a streetcar dispatcher, a liquor vendor, that one is Canadian. Then, for a moment, there is a sense of unity stronger than that between chance-met citizens of the same country, a heart-warming thing of pride and happiness that works constantly back and forth across the full length of the border, lovely and rich and strange, precious because it is not based on logic or advantage or anything except an emotional faith that never explores or questions itself. In the United States a Canadian is always a little better and bigger than life size unless or until he proves himself less, and an American in Canada is the same.

Canadians are not great flag wavers—we have no flag to wave, no ânthem we have learned to sing with true conviction. We wish for both and make great argument about them, but these things do not come by wishing. They grow from a nation's deeds and hopes and fears, too often from blood and strife and suffering. Perhaps Canada has not yet asked enough of her people—mostly, it seems, she has given. Britain has asked blood and service through a thousand years, has had both without stint, and has given greatly in return. America grew her flag on the blood of her own, in the strife of her union. Perhaps Canada attained unity too easily. Yet I sometimes think that she may find she has earned her emblem in the triple scarlet maple leaves of World War II. If so, let it be against a white ground, for the snow we are no longer too proud to admit and for my country's innocence.

Because I am not a native Canadian I thought it well to ask one of my daughters, "Do you think Canada is a good country?"

"Of course it is."

"Why?"

"Because it's a young country, not all used up. It's got a long way to go." She thought for a moment. "It's a good outdoors country—there aren't too many people. It's a varied country, two oceans, mountains, prairies, lakes, and forests. The United States will have to come to Canada more and more for everything, because they are using up all they've got."

"What else?"

"Well, it's got the old, old things in it, historical things. Quebec is an old thing in itself. Canada has a lot of history and then it's got new places, like Vancouver, grown up so quickly."

"What about Canadian laws?"

"Except for duties and things like that," remembering an unhappy moment in the customs, "Canada has good laws. Not too many restrictions. There's no segregation in Canada."

"Anything else?"

"Canadian jobs don't pay as well as American, but they're likely to be more interesting. They aren't so set—there's more future in them."

That seems a very modern, very rational statement of love of country, yet the essential convictions are there. It is a loyalty without historical fears or hatreds, without sense of guilt or false pride. It is the sort of loyalty that can be taken to world councils and used effectively within them for effective world government. It is not likely to respond to jingoism; it will be able to yield, yet will never accept domination or oppression.

I do not wish to claim perfection for Canada. My daughter

said, "There is no segregation in Canada." There is not. In large ways Canada shows greater tolerance towards minorities than any country I know. Yet Canadians are the most intolerant people I know. Almost any Canadian has a pet intolerance, probably several, that he will expound upon at a moment's notice. I have heard Canadians hating Catholics, Jews, Americans, Irish, English, Scottish, Ukrainians, Poles, Japanese, Chinese, French-Canadians, English-Canadians, Germans, Mennonites, Doukhobors—the list, for all I know, may cover every nation, race, religion, and activity on the face of the earth. It is so comprehensive, in fact, that one might be tempted to argue safety in it. But it is not a safe thing. Intolerance is a habit and it can be used. In parts of Canada intolerance is already dangerous. Vicious exchanges between Ontario's Protestants and Quebec Catholics lessen the nation. Prairie hatred of Ukrainians is often vicious and dangerous. Pacific Coast hatred of the Japanese, founded on economic jealousy, used the war to strip them of homes and property and liberty; there is no comparable shame in Canada's history.

I am not happy about Canada's treatment of Canadian Indians. It was benevolently conceived, paternalistic, in some degree protective; but it is hopelessly outdated, it is narrow, based on ignorance and misconception, and at this stage of the twentieth century it is oppressive. I think Canadians know this and that Canadian Indians will in time be given a new place in the country. But I think the change is long overdue and that every delay is shameful to us.

I am afraid for the unity and greatness of a country that trusts its civil liberties to the petty legislatures of ten provinces. I am ashamed that for this reason Canada cannot speak as a nation on human rights in the council of nations. I believe that a nation whose central government does not stand always ready to define and protect the human rights of its citizens must be unsure of itself and short of true greatness.

I think of Canada as a country that has never had and never needs to have a proletariat, in the Old World sense of a vast population whose lives are confined to dependence and drudgery. Yet there is danger that something of the sort may be produced synthetically, as much by the negative slowness of big business to share profits as by the determined efforts of those who believe they might win power through the existence of a proletariat. There is a type of immigrant mind, usually from the oppressed countries, that clings to conceptions of servility and dependence and refuses to look for the scope and greatness that is in Canada. It is a mind easily trapped and deceived into hopelessness, and I believe that the nation would do well to show itself more clearly to its new citizens. Business, still lost somewhere in the archaic mists of nineteenth-century capitalism, is fully as blind to the real meaning of Canada as the dullest of immigrant minds. A hundred years ago scarcely anything in Canada was owned in the Old World sense—it lay there, waiting for discovery and use. To have shared the profits of discovery and use honestly and fairly from the start would have made a proletariat forever impossible and built a country unlike any other on the face of the earth. It is still not too late for this.

These are political and economic matters for the most part and none of them is a lost or dead issue. They are things that Canadians think about and towards which the country is working, however slowly and gropingly. Politics and economics are not, thank God, a country; they may limit it or change it to some extent, but they do not make it. A country is the life and thought of the people who live there and I believe that Canadian life is as honest and fair and soundly based as the life of any people on earth. It is without bitter hatreds or savage jealousies, it is young, perhaps a little uncertain of its destiny, but it is courageous and active life and it has those qualities of urgency, flexibility, independence, and change that lead to creative development in the broadest sense. Without discarding or slighting the true worth of the past, Canada has freed herself from the limitations and failures of the past. She is not bound by fear or lethargy and has not bound herself in the overeagerness of immaturity. She has chances to learn that other nations have not had; she has a vigorous, aggressive, yet stable people and a great broad land to put that learning to creative use.

And when all this has been said, how little has been said. A country is not words, but feeling; not logic, but an idea and much faith. It is revelation, participation, experience, and heritage. Its realization comes in strange, sharp moments—entering a harbor in a great ship, seeing the city along the shoreline; poling a canoe against broken water among green timber; standing on a height, looking out over the land; in a way of speech or a recognition of thought. These are the simple, intensely emotional, almost physical ways, when the breath draws sharply and the mind knows in brilliant clarity of feeling. There are subtler, more complex ways, as when one talks in a group of Canadians, men who know the country intimately and work in the raw industries that make it. No one says: I am a Canadian. If anyone thought to name the thing at all he would say, more nearly: I work here. It is in the pace and mood of Canadian cities and in all the Canadian symbols the cities seem to deny—the buffalo head of the RCMP, the beaver of the Hudson's Bay Company, the ram's head of the Rocky Mountain Rangers, the cougar of the Seaforth Highlanders. It is in the Canada goose and the trumpeter swan, in the polar bear and the sea otter and the marten.

For Canada, in spite of the strip of settlement along her

southern borders, is still a country of gigantic wilderness. Even here, on Vancouver Island, where half a century of uncontrolled logging has stripped timber from millions of acres, wilderness comes back as soon as the axe passes—the logging roads grow up to alders, vultures and ravens and hawks wheel over the blackened miles behind the fires, the grouse nest on the hillsides and deer shelter in the thickets and swamps. The far north is the far north still, as anyone who has seen it knows: endless miles of scrub timber and muskeg, huge lakes, great rivers, then the barrens reaching to the Arctic Ocean and the polar land masses beyond. Infinitesimally small in it, scattered every three or four hundred miles along the rivers and the arctic coastline, are the outpost settlements. It is not a tamed country yet, nor likely to be for hundreds of years. Even Quebec is not all tame yet, nor New Brunswick nor the forests and waterways of northern Ontario. The country's true life is still in logging settlement and mining village, in prairie farm and stump ranch, fish camp and trapper's cabin, though the yield of all these and their needs funnel in to make the wealth of the cities.

There are those who speak apologetically for Canada, who claim that she is not yet a nation, that she lacks cohesion and faith in herself, that she has neither art nor literature, nor any real being distinct from her origins. I am not of these people; I have no feeling for them or with them, nor any faintest understanding of the self-depreciation that moves them. Whenever I have come to grips with the life of Canada I have found it strong and solid and real, the true, fresh growth of a vigorous civilization, neither contemptuous of its roots nor limited by them. McGill, Toronto, Dalhousie, and the other great universities are not the schools of a nation that doubts itself; there is nothing feeble or second-rate about the contributions of Canadians to medicine and biology and physics;

and when it was necessary to fight a war Canada found men and equipment to fight it in such a way that to be a part of her was a privilege.

Only a fool would resign his right to be critical of his country, its laws and beliefs and government; they must reflect an honest citizen in strong measure or he must seek to change them. I want change in Canada, and growth; but I trust myself to the country's present and my children to her future with a faith I could not have elsewhere.

Probably my own profession is the one most frequently attacked when faint-hearted Canadians are decrying their own country. There is, they repeat with monstrous persistence, no Canadian literature. I wonder: how do they know, these little magazines and small-time columnists and occasional amateur reviewers? Chaucer alone did not make an English literature, Thoreau, Whitman and Melville together are less than an American literature. The important thing is that there are Canadians writing and writing well, from Canadian minds, with Canadian faith and understanding. What we find to say is what there is, now, to be said. Perhaps those of us who are writing today are as the pioneer is to the dairy farmer, the fur trader to the industrialist. If so, I chose this and am content with it. It is good to be writing at the start of a country's history instead of at the end, to be looking on new unwritten places and new unwritten people, trying to understand, trying to find shape and pattern and meaning where none has been found before. There is no limiting tradition at such a time, no need for precious form or pretty experiment. There is only the subject, too vast to be seen clearly, too amorphous to be pressed into completely recognizable shape, an infinity in which to search and reach and feel for finite things. It is a freedom beyond all conceivable freedoms, bounded only by the imagination's reach and the mind's skill in finding words for it. If there can be no full success, if neither we who write nor the times we write in are ripe for profound understanding, at least we are in and of the country's flood, her spring, her increase.

Canadians may have to wait a while for their country to build a mass of past glories heavy enough to pack into recognizable shape. In the meanwhile they can live with her, in the awkwardness and grace of growth, in the splendor and strength of newness, heroes rather than historians.

APRIL

THERE IS NO BETTER TREE THAN the broadleaf maple of the Pacific Coast to draw the migrant birds in spring. The hummingbirds are among the first, finding the tree's abundant sugar in the pale, pendent flowers that put out before the leaf is fully sprung from its sheath. They quarrel and scold among themselves, flash angrily back and forth, hover and dart and perch. I think they perch more often now than later, perhaps because their powerful chest muscles cannot work their wings so easily in the cooler weather. Perching, they reveal themselves: rufous throats and the iridescent glory of their tiny backs.

The great three-trunked maple at the back door spreads its branches across the kitchen window, where we eat most of our meals. The scarlet hawthorn is just beyond it and two tall balsams are across the driveway; under these are spireas and mock orange and other shrubs as well as a small tangled herb garden, so the birds move almost constantly across the window. The hummingbirds are there early in April, a concentration of them, probably still in migration, though they pause for several days before passing on or spreading about the garden. The purple finches come almost immediately after, then the wild canaries, females and juveniles, hanging upside down on the maple blossoms and pecking at them. One seldom sees the adult males at this time; they appear later and gradually, at first one or two like clear gold lights among a dozen or more of the grey-brown females, then more and more until the numbers are about equal.

White-crowned and gold-crowned sparrows come early in the month, but they are seldom in the tree, seeming to prefer the hedges and shrubs, and the seeds and other feed they find on the ground. The woodland warblers show briefly in the maple when they first arrive, late in the month, then go off to their nesting and fly catching.

The band-tailed pigeons come back in April and I usually see them first as I am cleaning up the border; they fly from the alders behind the barn field, past the Balm of Gilead tree, and across the river. Later they come to the balsam trees in the evenings, bending the tips of the limbs far down and scattering pollen in golden clouds of dust as they search for something in the flowers. Occasionally they flutter their wings to regain balance or move position, and the dark bands of their tails and the purple breast and head show strongly in the long evening light.

It is impossible to watch birds in North America without remembering Audubon. Groupings, attitudes, colorings that he recorded with such deep perception are endlessly repeated by descendants of the birds he watched. The perching of chickadees, the curve of a swan's wings, blue jays on ripening corn, the flaunt of a merganser's scarlet leg and foot, the spread of a flicker's tail feathers, he has caught them all so closely that in seeing them one feels Audubon at one's elbow. I feel this, I think, with the woodpeckers most of all, and especially with the great pileated woodpeckers.

"A bird of the deep woods," my bird book calls the pileated woodpecker, and this is true, though I've seen one on a telephone pole right down in the village. He is conspicuous in every way, large as a pigeon, black of wing and back at rest, showing his white underwing in flight; white at neck and throat, with a strong black bar cutting back across his head from the eye; above this line, head and handsome crest bright scarlet. His cry is a wild laugh, confident and joyful. His flight dips and surges on intermittent wingbeats; it is as distinctive as his scarlet crest. His beak is long and sharp, and powerful enough to cut through two or three inches of green tree to get at the grubs in the rotten heart; it scatters chips that might have come from a man-made tool and leaves a gouged surface that could almost be the work of beaver's teeth.

I heard them laughing back in the alders as I walked towards the house from milking one day this month and, knowing their flight is often across the pasture to the big fir, hoped I might be lucky enough to see one. They came just as I reached the house, not one but four, across the road, across the pasture and into the maple tree, twenty feet from where I was standing. They dipped to it, perching here and there on the three trunks, claws rasping on the bark, scarlet heads cocked, and eyes bright. One spread his wings and held them spread. Another, higher on the same trunk, peered round at him. The bird with the spread wings moved upwards a little, the tapering, sharply pointed feathers of his woodpecker tail fanned out and gripping the tree to steady him. For a minute or two all four were moving about the tree trunks in patterns and posturings of black and scarlet. They did not feed, or fight, or even come very close to each other; yet they all seemed to be adult birds and I think the whole thing was a part of mating play. Two left the maple, one following the other towards the big fir. The other two left later, at longer intervals, looping down to cross the river. That is the only time I have ever seen four of the great woodpeckers together, and in the minutes I watched them they reproduced every pose of the Audubon plate.

One mating flight that Audubon does not record, though I am sure he must have seen it, is that of the bald eagle. I have seen it only in April, and only at the mouth of the Nimpkish on northern Vancouver Island. Against a blue sky, on a windy day, two eagles circling and circling, very high over the tide flats. Broad black wings, black bodies, heads and tails brilliantly white in the sunlight. One bird swings away and soars in easy circles, climbing two or three hundred feet above the lower bird. For a little while they sail serenely on the updrafts, seemingly unaware of each other. Then the upper bird swoops down, straight for the other, purposefully, at enormous speed. In the last second of time before the reaching talons strike her, the lower bird flips on to her back. Talon grips talon and they whirl together, with spread wings, over and over and over in wild, sweeping somersaults. The rush of air against their wings grows louder and louder until the sound fills the whole air and the wheeling bodies against the sunlit sky become a threat to the watcher on the tide flats below them. Then sharply, only fifty or a hundred feet above his head, they separate and climb away, wings still sounding against the air.

Migrant birds in the maple buds, sun and wind and clean air over the tide flats and the rush of eagle's wings. The scarlet, forceful thrust of peony and false Solomon's-seal from the earth, the vivid fresh green and lovely yellow of skunk cabbage above the black ooze of the swamps, flowers along the freshet-swept banks of the river, pink and white erythronium, green-collared trilliums, the compound leaves of columbine and meadow rue. All these and the first mist of palest green through the tops of the alders are in April, whether the year is late or early. And they secure the year's change from winter.

LIVESTOCK

Ann DOES A LOT OF ECONOMIC planning and she aims primarily at a sort of current security— a low fixed overhead, I believe a business man would call it. This is economic wisdom of a high order in any woman married to a writer of books, and it seems to work out well enough to keep us, at most times, within calculable distance of solvency.

The solid, unalterable base of all the planning is the cow. The chickens enter into it, of course, and so does the garden and the orchard and even my fishing and hunting. The sheep, I suspect, do not; if they earn their keep at all it is by eating down the grass and keeping the place reasonably tidy, and even this good work is dearly bought if one counts against it the roses and border plants and trees they manage to destroy whenever someone leaves the wrong gate open. There are also mechanical aids to economy: a planned kitchen, automatic dishwasher and automatic clothes washer instead of hired help. And a general principle, which includes myself as a carpenter and plumber and ditchdigger and Ann as a painter and decorator, of "Don't hire anything done if you can do it yourself." Essentially pioneer economics, in spite of electricity and the dishwasher. And that brings it right back to the cow again as the most important single factor.

Before I was married I was, like most woodsmen, very sensitive about doing farm work. In the circles I moved in it was considered the height of unwisdom to learn to milk a cow or to admit the skill if one had it. Far too often one was staying at a stump ranch where there were cows: cutting wood, hauling water, mending fences, even pitching hay, were acceptable tasks; milking cows was avoided if possible. When I was planning to get married I had to find a house and I decided to try and talk my friend and present neighbor, Reg Pidcock, into renting his. He was not easily persuaded, even into an experimental renting while I was still single. He made one final difficulty.

"Who'll milk the cow?"

"You can," I said. "You'll be around."

Reg also is a woodsman and I should have been warned by the change in his tone. "No, I won't. I'm going off fishing. You can learn. Go on out and milk her now."

I wanted the house, so I learned to milk. When Ann came up with me six months later we found we had the house and Reg's entire herd of four cows and their various offspring in our charge. Fortunately only Blackie had to be milked regularly and she was a gentle and pleasant creature, a Shorthorn-Jersey cross, well past her best years and with an easygoing way about milking times that more productive cows have not. I milked Blackie once a day, when I got around to it. The pasture was across the road and Blackie was usually somewhere well back in the bush behind it. But when I felt milking time coming on, I could yell from an upstairs window and she would probably come bounding out of the bush, her head with its one crooked horn shaking fiercely to keep the flies away. She would stand to be milked anywhere and she varied in all four quarters; I think it was the far hind quarter that did best and so took longest. The near front quarter was a dandy; two or three half-hearted squirts and you could call it milked; some while before we lost her it dried up altogether. I liked that quarter.

The other cows, Maggie and Jessie and one whose name I forget, were farmed on a somewhat different principle. Their duty was to raise calves with a minimum of trouble to all concerned, and when we first arrived they were doing just that; I had to pitch some hay down to them every day until the grass began to grow in the spring, but the calves did the rest. And when the grass began to grow, cows and calves wandered away up the road and into the bush and were seldom seen all summer.

But there came a time, inevitably, when the old calves had been butchered and new calves were to be born. Reg mentioned it quite casually, in the course of saying good-by as he was leaving for a couple of months in California.

"Maggie and Jessie are liable to calve while I'm gone," he said. "Better get them in a bit ahead of time."

"O.K.," I said unguardedly. "Anything else?"

"Just watch them when they calve. Milk 'em out for the first week or two, until the calf gets going."

"Milk them?" I asked with belated suspicion. "Have you ever milked those brutes?"

"You can't let a cow die from milk fever," Reg said. "You won't have any trouble."

Jessie was a wild-eyed creature, mainly reddish-brown, with strawberry-roan patches here and there. She already had her calf when I found her and looked as though she had had it for at least a month. I could see no signs of any trouble and she quickly made it clear that she didn't want me anywhere within several cow's lengths of her udder. I discussed it with neighbors and they agreed that Jessie had done it several times before. She would probably survive without any attention from me. But Maggie—now Maggie was a different matter altogether. Better watch her.

Maggie was a gigantic, raw-boned, muscular black and white Holstein, horse-high and with none of the placidity of expression one has a right to expect of a cow. I got her into the pasture before her time and kept watch with a heavy sense of responsibility. She had her calf during a wet and stormy night and I found her with difficulty the next morning, back in the bush behind the pasture. Her udder was splendidly swollen and it seemed to me that here, if ever, was a case of get the cow milked or lose her. After a few weak attempts to drive her, I grabbed the calf. It bawled and Maggie whirled in fury, her heavy horns stopping just short of the calf and me. Then she licked the calf with a great rasp of her tongue. In spite of the formidable nature of the gesture, I thought I could detect a motherly interest in it, so I started off with the calf. I got twenty or thirty feet away, calling, "Maggie, come along, old Maggie, good old Maggie," and other such insincerities before anything happened at all. Then the calf wriggled and blatted and Maggie came thundering after it. From then on it was a chase through the wet brush, with the calf bawling occasionally and Maggie breathing hard down my neck and seeming bigger every minute. We got to the barn at last and to my surprise she went into a stall and let me chain her.

I set the calf up near her head and moved in cautiously with the bucket. She kicked at once, with speed, accuracy, and power. There was a sideways throw to the kick, compounded of meanness and improperly aligned hind legs, which caught me on the knee, knocked me off the stool, and sent the bucket spinning across the stall. I tried again and the same thing happened, except that I managed to get myself and the bucket in the clear. About four kicks later, just as the bottom of the pail was covered, she landed her huge hoof over the rim of the pail. The kick's backwash wrenched the pail away from me with an enormous clatter, catching my fingers between the handle and the rim. Then she jumped on the pail with both hind feet, squashing it down into a compact mass of bright tinware, with many gleaming faces. My fingers came free from the ruin. I milked her out onto the floor of the barn and she stood through the whole process without a sign of protest.

Yet somehow, between Maggie and Blackie and Jessie and the other whose name I forget, I came to like cows. We moved from Reg's house to our own and so won free of any direct responsibility for the beef herd. But Blackie seemed to come along with us and she remained with us almost until we bought our own first cow, a lovely pale Jersey named Tulip.

Tulip was the sort of cow that wise dairymen hang onto, but she had been set back by the birth of twin bull calves and was milking below the standard of the herd, so we were able to get her. Not only that, but she had been bred to a Jersey bull of excellent repute and her first calf was a heifer, which we kept and named Heather. We had hired help for a while then and let the herd grow rather fast. Fern came, a dark Jersey of good habits, and after her Lupin, another dark Jersey who had had her second calf in the bush and was sold as a wild and doubtful prospect. She pitched out of the truck that brought her like a rodeo steer, ran into a rock and half stunned herself. I spent the rest of that evening trying to put a rope on her to milk her. Towards dusk, in desperation, I took the pail and settled down beside her right out in the open field. She stood through the whole process without a kick or move or a flick of her tail, and from then on we kept ropes away from her and had no more trouble.

By the time Heather was ready to freshen for the first time

the war was on, the hired help had left, and there was no more to be found.

"We sell the cows," I said.

"We keep one," Ann said.

"Ridiculous," I said. "I can't waste time milking cows. I've got books to write."

But we kept Heather. She was pale, like her mother and the bull that bred her, a creamy buff. She had long, sharp horns and a quick eye, and she was neat and dainty on her feet as a deer. She was quiet and friendly, yet never dull and always beautiful. When the time came for me to go to the army I said regretfully, "I guess we'd better sell Heather."

"No," Ann said. "I'll learn to milk."

"You can't do it, with a house and the children to look after and no one around."

"You can't feed children properly in wartime unless you do keep a cow," Ann said.

So she learned to milk and we kept Heather and I went away. When Heather calved in 1944, Ann wrote that she seemed dull and miserable for several weeks after calving, but picked up later. She had another calf in April of 1945, just before V-E Day, and the blue air-mail letters said again that she was sick and weak and listless, then that she had died. Reg came over and did an autopsy before he buried her and found a darning needle encysted in the muscle of her heart. It seemed to me that that had been a good heart, strong and brave beyond anything one would expect of a cow.

Ann doesn't hold theories for the sake of holding them. She borrowed a cow from a friend, a large and wise old crumple-horned cow named Tillie. Heather's calf lived and was a heifer, so Ann raised it on Tillie's milk and named it Primrose.

When I got home early in 1946, Tillie was still here and

Ann still had a place for cows in the economy. But Tillie is a cow of very strong character and her crumpled horn is a tool and a weapon that sets her apart from most other cows. She also has a talent for leadership and a power complex that never relaxes. I found that she had Primrose, who was by this time a well-built yearling heifer, so thoroughly terrorized that she would not come into the barn. Outside the barn Tillie's crumpled horn battered at her relentlessly whenever she was within reach. Tess, another and much larger cow that had come with her, was similarly terrorized, though Tillie tolerated her in a far corner of the barn at milking time.

Among cows, as among chickens and sheep and other gregarious creatures, this violent self-assertion and sharply graduated tolerance through the herd or flock are standard things, socially accepted and presumably socially useful. Primrose, as she grew, would undoubtedly have forced from Tillie a greater measure of tolerance and respect; in time she might even have established her right to pride of place in her own barn. And I might have excused Tillie and allowed her to stay on with us.

But Tillie was no mere figurehead; she led to real and positive purpose. As a tool the crumpled horn was infinitely versatile. It served as wrecking bar and crowbar, as battering ram and clawhammer, as pry and wrench and rasp. Tillie did not build fences, but she took them down and led the herd out over them with remarkable skill. She did, I think, close gates at times, but only in a defiant gesture; her main concern was to open them, by skillful manipulation of the crumpled horn if that availed, but ruthless force if it did not. I accepted the challenge and fought back for a while, strengthening fences and wiring gates until it was about as easy to move from one field to another as to escape from a concentration camp. Then she learned to open the little door that led into the feed bins.

The first problem that she solved was a simple hook and screw eye. I put a bolt on the outside of the door, but the crumpled horn took that out by the roots. Two bolts on the inside of the door were equally ineffective, so I put on a heavy padlock hasp. At first I considered securing it with a strong padlock, but it seemed likely that the crumpled horn would serve also as skeleton key, so I used a wooden peg instead. That held her or else she decided that dairy feed was not worth the effort.

Two nights after this was settled she led her herd across the pasture to where I had wired five heavy poles across a gateway. She removed the poles, one by one, and crossed another pasture to a fine picket fence designed to protect Reg's garden against anything that moved on four legs, from bears to dogs, from horses to hogs; but not from Tillie and the crumpled horn. In one calm and calculated sweep she ripped half a dozen pickets away from the fence, then led the herd into a glorious night of browsing and sampling.

So we passed Tillie on to another friend and that brings us down to our present state, with Primrose in full ownership of the barn and the barn field and the alder thicket behind. Tillie comes back occasionally and breaks into the pasture instead of out of it, but even those visits have been reduced a little since the village brought in a pound law.

Primrose, unlike her mother and grandmother, is a dark-colored Jersey, but she is small and neat on her feet as they were and even quicker with her sharp little horns. With Tillie gone it seemed for a while that she would carry on Tillie's tradition of leadership by dominating everything around her, chickens, dogs, barn cats, and attendant humans. But she was no match for a veteran who had warred with Maggie and Jessie and we soon came to a satisfactory working arrangement. She is still a lively little cow, quick to toss her head and bluff anyone who will be bluffed, but she comes quietly to the barn at milking time and stands quietly through it without chain or stanchion until the milking is done. She moves her feet at a spoken word or to a gentle pressure on her leg. She has large and comfortable teats and a yielding bag; when she is fresh she gives over four gallons of milk a day, and she holds up well through the toughest winter. When she must kick—and she never does without good reason—she gives a warning flinch and tries to avoid both the milker and the bucket.

Ann's wartime experiences with them confirmed her in a love for cows and barns and milking time that transcends mere economics, so we share the thing between us—I milk in the mornings, Ann at night, unless some exigency of domesticity prevents her. I still question the economics; feed bills mount up very quickly and it's wonderful how much time one can spend on a cow. And I resent milking when, as often happens, it interferes with something else I have to do and want to do. But it is also true that I enjoy milking nine days out of ten. The simple routine is both a relaxation and a stimulant. Walk over to the barn, along the path through the birch trees and across the road. Feed grain to the chickens, shake down laying meal in the hopper, check the chicken house and collect the eggs. Back in the barn, put dairy feed in the manger and hear the clatter of the bucket echoed by Primrose's quick step coming into her stall. Wash the udder with warm water and feel the milk flow down to swell the teats. The stool and the milk bucket. Milk drumming onto the bottom of the pail. A pause to put some in the barn cat's dish before the chickens can come up from their grain and chase her away from it. Perhaps children watching as hands work and foam builds deep on milk in the pail.

At the start of the day the mind is quick and live on whatever lies ahead. Problems solve themselves, the difficult sentence works itself out, the new chapter comes into shape. So many people have stood or leaned or squatted beside me when I've been milking—old Senator Evans, Alec Crawford and Johnny Holt, Julie Morris and Dolly, Will and Martha Ensley, Curly Blake, Mildred Hanson, Colin Ensley; Colin Ensley most of all. They've grown there beside me in the barn and worked their problems out or met their failures until they are always ranked behind me at milking time, ready to come forward at a flick of Primrose's—or is it Heather's or Fern's or Tulip's—tail or a movement of her feet.

Evening milking is relaxation from the day's demands and a purification—a clean and valid restoration of humility. Milking a cow is reality; it is fundamental, utterly important, an age-old human task. Too many things can happen in the course of a day to destroy a man's sense of proportion. There are little triumphs and successes, the too easy praise that one takes to oneself all too easily. People come, more humbly than they should, to ask advice or help. One sits in court, attended by magnificent men in uniform, and dares to judge one's fellow men. Those things swell in a man as they should not, build his petty self-importance as he would not have them build it. The quiet half hour in the barn on a still summer evening or with a winter storm flickering the lantern light changes all this, sets it back in proper proportion. The important delegation no longer seems so important—or so flattering. It will go its way and in time attain its little end, helped maybe to the extent of a pail of milk by what I have been able to tell it. The powerful arguments of the lawyers seem frail and devious beside the solidity of Primrose's golden flank; the wise decision, arrived at after so much close attention and careful thought, seems shallower in its wisdom when set against her fragrant warmth and the calm yield of her quiet day. Thought searches back over the day, humbly and honestly, detecting the false values and vain imaginings, stripping away protective dignity, revealing values and proportions that pride concealed.

TREES

IN A CONIFEROUS FOREST, AFTER a long spell of trapping or cruising, I begin to think I hate trees. Any swamp or lake or mountain slope, any open place at all becomes a haven of light and space, freedom from the overpowering density of evergreen and the enclosing trunks of the forest's infinity. Many of the pioneers felt this and fought timber with as much intensity and determination as they fought Indians and wild beasts and climate. In any country that was once forest, a contempt for trees carries over far beyond its purpose into years of wanton and brutal destruction. Here on the Pacific Coast high rainfall and swift regeneration do much to repair destruction. But here also the evils of machine logging have reached a peak of ruthless efficiency and set conditions for immensely destructive fires where fire should have been only a minor problem. And the bulldozer and the power saw have allowed the later settler to strip acres with an ease and speed the pioneer never knew. They inherit a dead and barren philosophy, these late-comers, as most of them realize and regret when the last tree has fallen and the last stump is wrenched away.

For the woodsman never hates trees for long, if he really hates them at all. And the pioneer is the first to resent the brutal stripping of the forest by the loggers who follow him. His own struggle was for breathing space and for light to grow his needed crops. He recognizes the attack of the loggers for what it is: a heedless destruction of the land for a brief, uneconomic profit.

The struggle of the pioneer against the deep forest is almost a history of civilization. Land that supports a mass of trees has little left for the support of other life and yields that little grudgingly, so man peopled the plains early and swiftly but established himself against the forest only slowly, as his tools improved and his skill increased. So the pioneer's struggle is a real one, spurred by determination to survive. But as soon as survival is assured he turns from his hatred of trees and begins to plant trees—trees for shade, shelter, ornament, and crop. And in this planting he finds, has always found, through his very nature a rich satisfaction and a deep pride. A tree is a bigger thing than a man and its span of life is far longer than a man's. Planting a tree is an act of faith little short of creation and it projects a man's hold upon the earth for as far beyond death as his imagination can reach.

The first planter of trees I ever knew was my grandfather, and he was one of the best. He planted trees around his houses, in orchards and walks, in shrubberies, and as single specimens. He encouraged the planting of trees in superb avenues that are now a feature of the town in which he lived. He planted rubber trees and tea-bushes, by remote control, in Ceylon. And he planted woods and coverts on the slopes of the dry chalk hills that he owned in England. There was a Victorian thoroughness in his approach to planting, and a Victorian complexity of motive. He thought of trees as a solid investment and a service to the country; he hoped his plantations would harbor pheasants and foxes, and he knew he would find pleasure in watching their growth; and he had a love of trees and a respect for them that transcended their usefulness or their beauty.

April

I knew grandfather best in his vigorous late seventies and early eighties. He was a small, spare, bearded man, upright and wiry, confident, dominating and dogmatic. Living in his house, we were supposed to respect his every wish. Being young and vigorous ourselves as he was old and vigorous, we did not always accept this theory wholeheartedly; at times we resisted to the point where violent word met violent word in shameless denial of the fourth commandment. Yet there were times when he tried, sincerely and ably, to teach us or help us; and in spite of our resistance across the wide gulf of years, he was often successful.

One duty that we had, and accepted none too gracefully, was to go with him on his walks. They were not long walks in distance—four or five miles, perhaps—but they were long in time, because the old man studied and loved his land and its use with a comprehensive knowledge of every phase of rural craft, from thatching to crop rotation, from the building of quickset hedges and dew ponds to the wise handling of meadow lands and skillful grazing of the uplands. So a walk was a succession of long halts, during each of which he expounded and explained—how and why a gatepost was wrongly set, why a field had gone back to docks and thistles, what was the history of this enclosure or hedgeline through the past several centuries. Sometimes what he said touched a live interest in us and we listened happily; more often we stood impatiently and sought unceasingly for some way to cut the lecture short and push the walk more quickly through its inevitable round. Yet many of the things he said lodged in our minds and became built into us.

He knew how and when and by whom the older woods had been planted, understood the health and value and purpose of their individual trees, and would go into all these things happily and at length. He taught us to recognize trees,

by bark and leaf and grain, and in spite of ourselves we grew
into some understanding of what he felt and meant. Occasionally we would show this, by a word or question, and the old
man's eyes would glance quickly up from under his thick grey
eyebrows and his lips would move in a rare, half-concealed
smile of satisfaction.

These older woods were hardwood stands, Tillywhim,
Longwall, Stonewall, Hangman's, of mature ash and beech
and elm and sycamore. But grandfather's greatest love was
for his own plantations on the slopes of the downs, orderly
woods of fifty or a hundred acres, curving round the contours,
solid, heavy green against the gorse and sheep-grazed grass
all about them. Here his knowledge was absolute, for he had
watched some of them through forty or fifty years, and often
their names recorded their planting dates—Jubilee, Coronation,
Great War, Prisoners of War. He studied them for growth,
for signs of disease, for the depredations of rabbits that had
found their way through the fencing; most of all he studied
the effect of them sweeping through the circle of the downs
—Prisoners of War, small and close at hand, Half Moon, its
forty-foot trees leveling a gully, Great War beyond that,
Coronation against the skyline, Kidney enfolding the dew
pond at the head of the valley, Forty Acres, Stratton Down,
Stratton Field, coming back to Newlands on the far side.
Conifers nursing hardwoods; Austrian pine, Japanese larch,
spruces, true firs, cedars, protecting oak and ash and beech,
drawing them up to clean-boled height before the great limbs
could spread and take over the wood. These, grandfather
knew, were his monument. At that time, between the two
wars, he could not have foreseen the changes that would come
to England and perhaps he imagined some descendant or successor standing where he stood to name the woods and their
planting dates to another, much later, brood of grandchildren.

That may not happen so far in the future as he would have seen it. In the changes the history of the trees and their planter may be forgotten. But the trees themselves will live their span and the woods he created from downland may well outlast many successions of trees. The falling leaves and needles will build up the shallow soil above the chalk and the tangled roots will hold the moisture on the hillsides. Whether a name be tied to it all or not, this is projection of a man's thought and action beyond his own mortality, a monument as vital as anyone could wish.

If I have written at length of grandfather's trees, it is because they have grown steadily in importance to me over the years. One of the first jobs I had in North America was scaling timber behind contract fallers. There was a double check on accuracy—the fallers themselves were directly interested, and the monthly totals had to come within a reasonable percentage of the water scale. It meant knowing the species, recognizing them quickly and accurately by bark, by grain, and by leaf. Not a difficult task, but the old man's training was a help and I remembered him. I remembered him again, many times, in the years I worked in the woods; loading logs, cruising timber, surveying, trapping or simply traveling, some feature of the woods, a species of tree I had not seen before, a habit of growth in a young tree, the way a broadleaf maple drew up to smooth-trunked height in a stand of conifers, recalled the plantations on the Dorset hillsides. While he lived I occasionally wrote him of such things and once or twice I sent him seeds of the great Pacific Coast trees—Douglas fir, Western hemlock, red cedar, Sitka spruce, white pine, and the true firs that we sloppily call larch or balsam. The seeds were planted and the small trees grew and were moved out to the hills before the old man died. No doubt they grow there still and will for a hundred years or more, their roots reaching out over the unfamiliar chalk to gather the Atlantic rains that drain down the slopes as swiftly as our own Pacific rains drain from the rock and gravel mountainsides of Vancouver Island.

When a Pacific Coast woodsman turns from trees he turns from evergreens, not deciduous trees. A stand of tall alders and maples along a river bottom is relief to him; even in summer the sunlight finds a way down through and between the leaves and there is life on the ground under them, growth of ferns and flowers and shrubs in the leaf mold. All this, like the graceful growth of vine maple and the carpet of creeping juniper in the hills, like the spread and slant of barberry and crab apple in the swamps, is sharp contrast to the heavy canopy of the true forest. Deciduous trees, even in heavy stand, are as exotic and restful to him as meadow or prairie or sand dune.

In spite of grandfather's early example, it had never occurred to me that I should want to plant trees. Yet when we bought this place, almost the first thing we did was to go out in the woods, dig up three broadleaf maples, and move them to our own land. I can't remember why it seemed so urgent to do this; nor, looking at the trees where they are now flourishing, the largest of them over thirty feet high and nearly two feet in circumference, can I see that they have filled any outstanding lack of shade or shelter or ornament. Perhaps it was simply a statement of ownership, for neither Ann nor I had ever owned a foot's breadth of land in our lives before. I feel them as such now and mark their swift growth and noble spread with a satisfaction that could only come from some such unpractical consideration as this.

As soon as the maples and ourselves were established by a year of growing into the place, I began more planting. My first choices were golden willows and birch trees, for the light and life of their bark in the winter months. The willows have never grown well for me, partly because the ground is not wet enough and partly because they are attacked by the diseases of the native willows. But the birches have given me the keenest pleasure of all the trees I have planted. They grow well and quickly in our sandy soil, they are always beautiful, and no two, even of the same species, have quite the same habit of growth.

I had supposed at first that birches were a fairly simple matter. I expected white bark, silk-smooth and patterned, with the sap blisters I remembered in the birches of my youth; slender, graceful growth, pale and delicate foliage. The only birch native to Vancouver Island is the Western birch, *Betula occidentalis*, a handsome tree and a strong grower, but heavier and coarser than I wanted. So I bought *Betula alba*, the European birch.

These grew well and, I noticed, with sharply varying habits; some more or less weeping, some upright, some shooting from the base, others spreading in top growth, some with many short branchlets, others with long and supple shoots. Then I discovered *laciniata pendula* which has perhaps the loveliest growing habits of all—narrow leaves, deeply serrated, a straight silvery trunk, strong yet slender main limbs, with branches weeping from them in such suppleness that the least breeze stirs them. The whole tree is wonderfully supple and flexible, bending so readily to summer or winter winds that one fears for it in heavy storms. Yet it always returns to straightness and symmetry.

From then on I began to learn about others—*purpurea*, with purple leaves and bark, *maxcimowicziana*, the great-leaved birch from Japan, *fastigeata*, of incurving growth, *nana*, the dwarf, *ermani*, from Asia, *papyrifera*, the canoe birch, and many others. Though I couldn't buy and plant all those I learned about, I felt that I was doing fairly well and that I might, in time, build up a pretty good collection. Then, on a hot Sunday afternoon during the war, I went to Kew Gardens. There were a lot of things I wanted to see there, but my most important concern was the birches; I decided tolerantly that I might learn something or I might perhaps have the even greater satisfaction of finding that I had something of which Kew knew nothing.

The first birches I saw were reassuringly ordinary—handsome specimens of *verrucosa* and *pubescens*. For a while I became interested in rhododendrons and madronas, a brilliant golden maple, great rough-barked sweet chestnuts, Mount Atlas cedars, and other wonderful things. Then I found birches again, a long double line of young trees at the edge of a wood. Each one was named and almost at once I knew my place— there was nothing I could show Kew. Three of the first labels I looked at read *B. schmidtii*, *B. japonica*, *B. ocoriensis*, all new names to me. I followed along the line and found yellow-barked *lutea* from eastern Canada and New England, then a dozen more that were strange to me. Looking ahead I saw another double line bordering another strip of woodland and humbly made up my mind that I would follow them all through the gardens, wherever they led me, trying to understand whence they came and why they were different, marking down only the names of the most attractive specimens, so that some day I might hope to round my collection into something approaching skeleton form.

I think I now understand my troubles; as a botanist I was being a fairly good ichthyologist. Ichthyologists have recently simplified their science by some good healthy lumping—they have, for instance, reduced the recognized species of trout from fifty or more to a comprehensible three. In my simplicity I had supposed that botanists, working in their own element, would be far ahead of fish men, but apparently their difficulties are still with them, especially among the birch trees.

Betula alba, I found, was named by Linnaeus. After him came Ehrhart, who split *alba* into *verrucosa* and *pubescens*, the common silver and the common white. From there in all is confusion to my amateur research. Ehrhart's *pubescens*, someone decided, is a variation of *glutinosa*, which someone else had previously named *pendula*. Even our Pacific Coast *occidentalis* had once been confused with the mountain birch *fontinalis* and the canoe birch *papyrifera*. And here I suspect even Kew, in all its wisdom, is still a little muddled, for I found in my wanderings that day a sapling clearly marked *B. papyrifera occidentalis*.

Nothing in all this has altered my love of birch trees. I still want the cut-leaf *verrucosa gracilis*. I want *fetisowii* of the pure white bark, orange-barked *macrophylla* and *albo-sinensis* (var. *Sepentrionalis*), the weeping *cripps* and the splendid *excelsa*. Meanwhile those I have grow each year to greater glory. *Laciniata pendula*, down by the river, lifts lacy foliage high against the summer sky; *tristis* weeps in cascades of summer green that ripple like a girl's skirts in the breeze and in winter the pendent, slender branches are like a girl's long brown hair thrown forward to dry; *ermani* stands straight and tapering as a pylon, trunk palest buff, limbs strong and black, leaves richly green until fall turns them overnight to guinea-gold.

Birches, of course, are hedonist's trees, beautiful, quick-growing, easily satisfied, of minor timber value, and short-lived. Fifty years from now the bravest of mine will be ready to lie down and die, unless some contractor's bulldozer has already torn it out by the roots.

I have planted soberly too. Poplars, limes, red oak, sweet chestnuts, walnuts, sycamores, horse chestnuts, sorbus hybrids, copper beeches, green beeches, even an English oak. And more recently, as though reconciled to the woods again, I have wanted evergreens—junipers, deodars, exotic cedars, and pines.

All this leaves out the flowering trees, dogwoods, crab apples, quinces, laburnums and lilacs, catalpas and false acacia, white, pink and scarlet hawthorns. And the orchard. And the native trees that survived the clearing or have grown up since. It seems a formidable list, yet we are not overpowered by trees, nor even sufficiently shaded and protected by them. In time I hope to plant the whole acre of Richardson's field and see it grow to cut the sweep of the southeast gales to a whisper. But I shall not be planting for shelter or for timber or for the future. And the birches have taught me that I shall never know very much about trees. I plant simply for the intimate pleasure of watching an individual tree's seasonal changes and its growth from year to year.

MAY

O<small>F ALL THE LIFE AND VIGOR</small> that temperate climate and heavy rainfall produce, none is more impressive than the massed shading greens of early spring growth, before maturity sets color and dulls contrast in leaf and blade and frond. There is delicacy and promise in this beyond that of the handsomest flowers, yet the beauty of flowers is in it and flowers themselves have a share, as do colors that are not green though they may be forerunners of green.

From the east windows of this room, in early May, there is a chance repetition of these colors of spring growth that gives quick expression to its essence: across the lawn, strong in the earth of the border, a thrust of scarlet peony leaves; behind them, clear white of bridal-wreath spirea; close behind that the dark green of the Douglas-fir hedge. Above the hedge are the red leaves of Japanese crab apple; distantly behind that and still above it, the white blossom of two yellow plum trees, then the darkest green of a spreading red cedar. This is forcing, straining, powerful growth, with depth and repetition that touches the senses and a burden of promise that reaches beyond the senses.

From this north window, this wide window by the desk, there is only green at that time, but green in infinity of shading and texture and quality. At a glance, it is massed tone and shade, piling up in rounded forms to the straight skyline of the high bank across the river. Then the eye turns into it and finds the true values. First the quince trees in the orchard, pale almost to blossom whiteness; then the cut-leaf birch by the edge of the river, still pale but a clear green, brilliant for all its delicacy. Across the river the maple flowers are pale gold, yet the color is still green, not yellow; the alders are heavier and stronger green and the willows among the alders are green of green, the one shade of all these greens that the eye knows for the color's own original. On the crest of the ridge the conifers have their deepest darkness of green, so absorbent of light that a dull day makes it close to blackness. And in places along the bank there is the white shine of dogwood petals that were green themselves until a few days ago.

Some of these are exotic greens, as the vivid green of the lawn is exotic and the soft green of the apple trees. One is inclined to expect strong effects from exoticism and to discount them, either from taste or in emotional preference for native things. But this is an effect of mass and volume, of a pervading and enormously powerful outthrust of living. The infinity of contrast is within it and of it, never an essential feature that stands out by itself. The mass is native, not exotic: willows, alders, maples, and the conifers give it depth and density, substance and extent. And the sharpest of the contrasts are native also: the scarlet bark of the ground-maple shoots and the pale clusters of their young leaves, yellow and scarlet of the willow switches, white of dogwood and thimbleberry blossom.

Somewhere during this time of the immature leaf there comes, every year, a day of blue-black clouds and pouring rain. The dull light of storm intensifies the greenness of every dripping leaf until one has the feeling of being underwater. It is wet underfoot and overhead, the whole air is saturated and heavy with moisture, there is wetness even between the raindrops. The clouds filter a heavy grey light on the world, but the shining, rain-washed leaves reflect it in greenness and light is transmuted to something more solid than air, with the lucent color of deep lake water over a weed-choked bottom.

On a day like this, and again it happens every year, either because the strange light makes them more noticeable or because they move more with the wetness, the wild canaries are suddenly everywhere through the greenness. For the first time the brilliant males are as numerous as the females. They drive across the lawn, strike the birch and the climbing roses along the fence and the apple trees beyond, cling there like golden fruit moving in the wind, chatter and change, pelt away with the wind and rain behind them, then suddenly are back. The vivid yellow of the rounded bodies is so clear and bright against the green that nothing else is yellow or gold anywhere around them, even though it seemed so moments ago. One accepts the gold as another wonder of the washed, underwater light and only later can realize the further contrast of the black face, the black and white wings.

May is a hurrying month, too good and full to last for long. For a little while everything has the lightness and clearness and cleanness of spring and the phallic thrust of sudden growth. Then, as though one had glanced away for a moment, the promise is realized and the fullness of summer is everywhere: the sap-filled shoots are hidden by leaves, scarlet of peony is green, the sooty catkins of the walnut are scattered and the leaves are out, the bloom of the dogwoods is over, the scarlet hawthorn has begun to fade.

The annual repetitions of May are so many that they tend to pass into the whole feeling of the month. But a few stand.

There is the unfailing hatch of winged, blundering black ants that comes faithfully in the first two really hot days of the month. In most years these hot days are in the last third of the month, not before the twentieth, not after the twenty-seventh, and I had supposed that they were the culmination of a long maturing process, coincidence rather than direct cause. This year was slow and late as a year can be, but the first two hot days of May came early in the month—the seventh and eighth—and the ants were with them. I am impressed with the ants particularly because I am a fisherman—as any fisherman knows, thousands of ants blunder to death by drowning on the surface of every lake and stream, and the trout come up to them as they do only to such unusual and bountiful manifestations—but I think anyone must find them impressive. They come so suddenly, and in such numbers, year after year. They spread so widely across the face of the land and so evenly, never in great concentrations, yet always in pouring numbers that chance seems to halt as individuals strike something or shed their wings or simply drop down in weariness. For two days they come in steady spread; for another day or two they are crawling almost everywhere; then they are scarcely seen for a whole year unless one disturbs a nest in a rotten log or builds a camp too close to the ground they work.

In May there is the ceremony of tying up the peonies. I try to calculate this carefully, so as to have to do it only once. After there is a good growth of leaf, but before the growth is full so that continuing spread will conceal the ties, and before a heavy storm can come to beat down the leaves. As a result I usually have to work in frantic haste with storm clouds already heavy in the southeast. It is pleasant work, probably the easiest, most dignified gardener's work I do all year, and it shows me the last recesses of my border as nothing else does.

Hummingbirds come as I work and hover at columbine blooms only a foot or two away; white-crowned sparrows and chipping sparrows are always nesting in the hedge behind the border then and they perch on the almond trees and the Japanese crabs to scold my nearness. Band-tailed pigeons sweep by in their strong flight, back and forth from their nests in the alders to their feeding across the river.

And always in May, below the lawn, at the very edge of the river, a chocolate-brown fritillaria lily blooms. It is frail and tiny, almost lost in the coarseness of orchard grass and salmonberry and wild rose that springs up there every year. Its bulb is often buried a foot or two under water in freshet time. Yet it has survived a dozen years in the same place since I have known it. For all I know it may have been there a hundred years, blooming always, with a gentle strength, in May.

COUNTRY MAGISTRATE
In Court

I HAVE BEEN A MAGISTRATE FOR about ten years now, to the deep amazement of my friends and my own occasional surprise. I came into the job in what seemed to me an extraordinarily casual way, simply because there was no one else around who wanted to take it on. My good friend Corporal Tennyson, of the local police detachment, told me this one day and asked if he could send my name forward to the attorney-general. I thought quickly of a dozen reasons why I was quite unfitted for anything of the sort; and at thirty I felt far too young—magistrates should be old and wise and grey.

"It's mostly by the book," the Corporal said. "And what

isn't written down is just common sense. You owe it to the country anyway—you've got the education and the time."

So, in due course, I became one of His Majesty's Stipendiary Magistrates in and for the Province of British Columbia, sworn to administer the law, doing "equal right to the poor and to the rich, after my cunning, wit and power."

I heard my first case on the day I took the oath. I sat at a desk, feeling small and confused, flanked by two magnificent policemen in the imposing uniform of the Provincial force. I listened to the Corporal's strong voice: "I declare this court open in the name of His Majesty the King." Then my own voice read out the charge. It was a simple matter, possession of an unregistered revolver, and the accused, I could see at once, was a badly scared man. That was the last thing I did see at all clearly for the next ten or fifteen minutes, while I tried to listen to the evidence for both sides. Every muscle in my body was suddenly rigid and no power or cunning I could exert would relax them. My hands shook, my eyes blurred, and my mind struggled with the spoken words as though they were a flood that would drown me. I got through it somehow, maintained a semblance of composure, spoke my verdict and the sentence. But it was a physical struggle that left me exhausted.

I won't profess to understand this reaction. It came upon me suddenly and unexpectedly, as stage fright or buck fever comes on people; it was like freezing at a high place in the mountains or with a canoe against white water. It has never happened to me since, yet it is never too remote from me on the bench. It is easy to name contributing factors: overanxiety, sense of inadequacy, excessive self-consciousness; but none of these tells the whole story. The act of sitting in formal judgment upon one's fellow man, for however slight an offense, is a formidable one. I never want it to seem otherwise, and though I can now hold my mind clear and my body calm through a case of almost any strain and difficulty, I should mistrust myself if I felt it less than an exacting task.

Because the appointment is so casual, because it does not call for legal training or any qualification more unusual than a fair local reputation for honesty and stability, it is natural enough to suppose that the work is not too difficult or too important. But in British Columbia the magistrate's courts deal with about 98 per cent of the criminal charges laid; in the remaining 2 per cent they make a close and formal examination of the prosecution case before deciding whether or not to send the accused to face a higher court. In other words, the magistrate's courts are the absolute base of the judicial system. They are the only criminal courts with which the general run of the public is likely to have any direct dealings. And it is upon them that the public will largely base its opinion of the judicial system it supports.

One reason for the casual form of appointment is that there must be many magistrates. It is an important principle of justice to limit a lower court's jurisdiction to as small a geographical area as possible, so that there may be no undue hardship on the defense in bringing witnesses or other evidence. And it is an essential right of any arrested person to be brought before a magistrate or justice within twenty-four hours of his arrest.

There is also an ancient conception of criminal law as something simple, conforming so closely to natural moral standards that it is best administered by the intelligence of individuals not too far removed in training and upbringing from everyday standards and ways. In Canada, great distances and scattered populations have always been a problem. The difficulty of finding suitable magistrates has at times been so great that members of the Mounted Police have been appointed justices or magistrates, and occasionally have sat in judgment on offenders they had themselves arrested.

Something of all this is carried over into the present system. The tendency is to assume that an ordinary citizen can be safely steered through the intricacies of procedure and the laws of evidence by the experience of police officers prosecuting in his court. He is given no preparation or guidance other than a barebones copy of the Criminal Code of Canada, and must ferret out for himself the other legal volumes that can help him. This tends to force an unnaturally and undesirably close relationship between the bench and the prosecutor, who is normally a policeman. Under frontier conditions the system may have worked fairly well. Under modern pressures, in a country that is moving out of the pioneer stage, it leaves far too much to chance. It is too easy for the bench to become little more than an extension of police powers. I think of a fisheries case where the magistrate heard the evidence and indicated that he would dismiss.

"But, Your Worship," said the prosecuting inspector. "What will the *Department* say?"

His worship nodded understandingly. "Have to think of that, of course. Guilty, I suppose. A hundred dollars and costs."

That was simple and straightforward. But much the same thing can happen very subtly, so subtly that only a man very finely tuned to himself could possibly be aware of it; something of the sort must always be a factor of risk when a magistrate is in any way dependent upon a prosecuting officer, because even the fairest and most honest prosecutor has a special interest in every case he presents.

The appointment of lawyers as magistrates is not, I am quite sure, the remedy. Lawyer-magistrates are necessary in the big cities, where they have full-time work and extended powers and can be paid worthwhile salaries; in rural areas lawyer-magistrates could only be inadequately paid and this would attract the incompetents of the profession, who hang on the edges of politics.

A highly trained legal mind is not necessary in a country magistrate, and it probably is not desirable. A magistrate must have a good knowledge of what is and what is not evidence; he must be familiar with the essentials of court procedure; and he should have a fresh and clear knowledge of the section of law with which he is dealing—something readily acquired by careful reading of the pertinent pages of three or four volumes that belong in every law library, however small. If he has this he will have more than most lawyers who argue in his court and he will be able to follow their arguments in comfort and confidence. And it remains true in a summary hearing no less than in a jury trial that a man has a right to be tried by mentality akin to his own, not specialized away from him.

It may seem that talk of procedure and laws of evidence tends away from this virtuous simplicity. Only rarely is a magistrate's court involved in fine points of law. Yet common sense alone is never enough to ensure a proper hearing. It is the business of the courts, even the simplest of them, to administer not merely justice, but justice according to law. The trouble with common sense is that one man's common sense may be another's damn foolishness. The law, especially criminal law, is the collected and amended common sense of hundreds of years and thousands of minds. British and Canadian law has been cumulatively calculated to protect an innocent defendant from conviction through prejudice, coincidence, pretrial abuses, or any other mischance that can be anticipated. But these protections exist only when rules of procedure and the laws of evidence are followed, and no wise magistrate will risk his own honor or an accused man's liberty without every protection the law grants both.

Only in this identification with the wisdom of the ages can a man in judgment upon his fellow man find any measure of security and confidence; understanding and using the framework that has been built for him, he is no longer simply a man, but a controlled and limited part in a system that has grown through the trial and error of thousands of years and dozens of civilizations. He is no longer free to act as he, a frail and simple man of one body and one mind, would act, but as the most carefully wrought concept of human justice would have him act.

Yet with all the protections that can be added to him, the man who sits in judgment is still a man and it is essential that he should be; he will need all the qualities of compassion, understanding, intelligence, and humanity that are in him. Whatever his protections, whatever his qualities, he will still have his prejudices and preconceptions fast in him, he will still be limited by the narrowness of his own experience, by the particularity of his own upbringing and his own way of life. The last measure of his worth as a judge will be in his ability to recognize these limitations, assess their intensity, and compensate for them.

Elkhorn was a quiet place when I first became a magistrate, but it has grown since then and I now hear two or three hundred cases a year. Many of them are minor matters of drunkenness or traffic violation, but I know that an appearance in court rarely seems a trivial matter to a defendant and I have learned also that there is no such thing as a routine case. No offense is ever committed twice in exactly the same way; every accused person differs from every other in thought, word and deed; and every one of them, in his own special being, is to himself the most important person in the world. A wise court, however inferior in the legal hierarchy, sits always with these points well in mind. Its first duty is to administer justice according to law and so safeguard the welfare of the community; after that its aim should be to satisfy both the accused and public opinion that justice has been done. No court can achieve all four objectives with unfailing regularity; no court is doing its duty except when it is attempting to do so.

It is inevitable that the only important person in any criminal court is the accused. No matter how brilliant the lawyers, how learned the judge, how significant the issue, no matter how silent or dull or difficult the accused himself may be, this remains true. For the accused man is the individual at odds with the state, and the state is seeking to affect his freedom. It can do so only at cost to itself; it can keep the cost bearable only by considering him at his utmost value, as an individual man, sacred to himself and as real to himself as any other man alive. When a state denies or fails to understand any part of this, it is attacking its own essence.

From this it follows that the mass of minor offenses can never be trivial to the state. In the mass they are well handled or badly handled, and citizens will gain their impression of the state's justice from this. Many people, especially the foreign-born, come to court expecting abuses. Not once, but many times, men asked to plead to a charge have said to me, in one way or another: "But, Your Worship (occasionally in flattering confusion, it is 'Your Majesty'), I must be guilty. Otherwise the police wouldn't have brought me here."

It is not always the uneducated or the foreign-born that say something of this sort, and the thing can be said with varying degrees of truculence or subservience. Neither attitude has a place in the courts of a self-respecting country, but it can be surprisingly difficult to convince a man that the court at this stage is interested only in his own opinion as to his guilt or innocence. If his defense is good and the charge is dismissed he often seems bewildered. In the case of a recent immigrant it may take several confirming experiences to convince him that his adopted government means him well, but at least the job is started.

The pettiness of nearly all crime still amazes me. One reads in the newspapers of "assault with actual bodily harm," "false pretenses," "indecent assault," "obstructing a police officer." The phrases are formidable and vividly descriptive; they seem to imply purposeful toughs planning and executing wanton violence and deceit. But when crime and criminal appear in court both are likely to look very different. The criminals are nearly always pathetic, harried, confused, and stupid. "Actual bodily harm" turns out to be a black eye and a few scratches; "false pretenses" is probably the signing of a worthless check for a few dollars in a harassed moment. "Indecent assault" came out of a drinking party, as likely as not; the girl had been encouraging all evening, the young fellow hopeful, finally a little too pressingly hopeful. "Obstructing a police officer"—drunk almost certainly.

There are real criminals, of course, and there is real crime; and occasionally both show up even in my court. But for the most part crime is a sad little thing, shoddy, explainable, less than vicious, almost never villainous. And the people who come into court are hard up or lazy, worried, frightened, foolish, sex-starved or hasty, but almost never wicked.

This is apparent only in the calm daylight. When the girl is being assaulted, the policeman obstructed, the check cashed, crime in its ordinary meaning is there; organized society is being attacked and must defend itself by its tried methods. So the pale and watery criminal appears in all his drabness before the bar of justice.

Ann says in moments of irritability that I believe them all

and all the stories they tell. Then I have to remember old John. Such a respectable, grey-haired old gentleman, slender, stooped, bespectacled, and mild. He had created a disturbance aboard a coastal steamer and was most apologetic about it. Yes, he must have had a drop too much. That would be easy —he wasn't used to drinking. And there was this good job up the coast, the first he had had in a long while. He had no money to pay a fine and it was so important to get to the job.

I arranged things so that he could do just that and added a few caustic comments about the failure of shipboard authorities to handle such a dear old gentleman, and the harshness of policemen who would hazard his job.

A few days later I was working my way steadily through several cases. I came to a charge of theft, read it, and looked up at a bedraggled, disreputable old man. Incautiously I asked, "Haven't I seen you somewhere before?", then caught the prosecutor's eye and realized that this was old John again. He was sorrowful and repentant as he had been the first time. Spectacles, collar, and tie were gone. The grey hair was ruffled, the eyes bloodshot, the respectable coat torn, the dark trousers stained and muddy. Yes, he was guilty. Must have been drinking again. I began to think of ways to get him up to his precious job. But the prosecutor was ready this time. He asked about previous convictions.

Old John scratched his head. There might have been something, some little thing, years and years ago.

The prosecutor read slowly through a list—theft, breaking and entering, armed robbery, theft—fourteen of them altogether and old John reluctantly admitted each one.

Much too soon after old John, there was the bright, well-dressed young man who had stolen a few boards from a lumber company to start building a house for his attractive young wife. He was contrite, his wife was tearful, and I gave him every benefit a first offender is entitled to. A month later the city police caught up to him with a list of theft charges that included everything from an automobile and a small yacht down to a shovel and a fountain pen. His list of previous convictions wasn't quite so long as old John's, but he had spent six of the preceding eight years in jail.

There have been, and there will be again, others like old John and the bright young man, and no doubt I shall believe in their respectability or simplicity or whatever it is they want me to believe in. Perhaps a country magistrate doesn't see enough old offenders to recognize them very promptly. But it remains true that real criminals, in the popular conception of the term, are very rare creatures. I have yet to meet one who comes up to the required standards as a willful, determined, and dangerous enemy of society.

I have known some very primitive men, most of whom were notably gentle and kindhearted under normal circumstances. Under adverse circumstances, when they are drunk or offended or embittered, these same men can be very dangerous. I remember a huge Latvian who died of burns not long ago after saving three lives in a fire. When drinking he usually remained sentimental and friendly, but sometimes he liked to fight and his enormous strength and his insensitivity to pain made him quite dangerous. He was powerfully and coarsely sexed and, again when drinking, might do and say things to revolt the toughest mind. There was a conviction against him for rape and several for minor crimes of violence. When his mother died, he spoke of her in pure poetry and wept for her with all the desperate sincerity of a child. Certainly he was dangerous and certainly he would have been more dangerous without laws to control him; but he was not essentially cruel or wicked or contemptible. At his best he was a very good man and a very useful one.

I think perhaps there is not and never has been a living man or woman who conforms exactly to the vague popular conception of what makes a criminal. The aggressive psychopath is probably closest to it, but even this deadly creature can be understood and treated and cured. True, the cost of treatment is excessively high and the end product will be nothing better than a fifth-rate citizen, but the mere fact that understanding is possible changes the whole picture. If understanding is possible, prevention is possible; and if prevention is possible, blame in the old sense and wickedness in the old sense no longer exist. Crime grows primarily from the unlucky circumstances and conditions which affect the complexity that is an individual man or woman; the future is not in penal therapy or any other panacea for the rehabilitation of criminals, but in anticipating and counteracting those influences that produce criminals.

The law, of its very nature, can only grow into a conception of this kind. It must change gradually as the conception proves itself on the level of everyday use and becomes part of society's conscience, because the law must never risk in abrupt change the inherited wisdom that separates it from tyranny. Some such gap as this always exists between the written intent of the law and the actual state of man's advancement in understanding of his fellowmen. Within the limitations set by law it is the function of the courts to bridge this gap, and almost inevitably they will tend to do so because a court is a man or group of men living and thinking in the present. A hundred years before Lombroso, Henry Fielding as a magistrate made a close, if prejudiced examination of environmental conditions producing crime. In the early nineteenth century the courts expressed the increased humanity of the times by using every legal loophole to avoid the savagely cruel penalties laid down by law. So a modern court, living and working in an age when human values are reckoned far ahead of property values, must do its best with a code that has not yet outgrown the insecurities of a society emerging from feudal restraints.

Not all affairs that come to court call for such complicated thinking. Many are settled in easy good humor. The Monday morning drunks often nod sympathetically, sometimes even apologize, as a policeman describes their week-end extravagances and the trouble they have caused him. Even assaults and disturbances can be affairs of great good humor. The affair of Ivan Cernoff and Mrs. Cernoff, who had made a shambles of a local restaurant, was almost pure comedy. Ivan is huge in every way, length, breadth, and depth, and his wife is as large, though not quite so tall; their combined weight would be something in excess of six hundred pounds. Ivan's face was badly cut and one eye was tightly closed by a fearful red and blue swelling. It had been a fine, uninhibited disturbance, with fists and dishes flying freely, a bowl of soup poured over a waiter, chairs and tables broken. Only Ivan's ruined face seemed unexplained. "How did that happen?" I asked him.

Ivan shrugged his great shoulders and there was a laugh from Mrs. Cernoff in the back of the courtroom. "I did it," she said. "I threw a water pitcher. Meant to hit the copper, but the old man caught it instead." Then they both laughed together, the complainants laughed, the prosecution laughed, the whole courtroom laughed. Clearly the disturbance had added up to a wonderful time, if one knew how to add properly. All the damage had been paid for, the Cernoffs had expressed things they needed to express, the police had done their duty satisfactorily and promptly. I set maximum fines, but only because the Cernoffs have such formidable means of expressing themselves that some restraint seems needed.

May

Many Indians appear in my court every year. They are rarely charged with anything more serious than having bought or drunk liquor. But an Indian case is never trivial. Indians come to court on these charges with a sense of injustice and discrimination. They are right. The laws that keep liquor from Indians were passed long ago, to protect them from the dirty trading practices of white men. Out of this has grown a myth, perpetuated by the ignorant and prejudiced, that Indians "go crazy" when they drink. I once heard a retired Mounted Policeman put that in its proper light. "Sure," he said. "A drunk Indian is tough to handle. Goes right back to a savage. He's liable to be just about as mean and ornery and dirty as a drunk white man."

It is not simply a question of liquor, but of freedom and the human dignity that belongs with freedom. I am ashamed every time it is the duty of my court to punish Indians for something that is a crime only for them. I am still more ashamed when I act on the law that forces me to ask an Indian where he got his liquor. The answer is nearly always the same in sum: a white man I have never seen before gave it to me; it was dark; I don't know what he looked like. I can believe the story and let the man go; or call him a liar and send him to jail. If there is anything in all this that adds to the honor of the court, the safety of the state or the dignity of the individual, I haven't yet been able to discover it.

There have always been and there always will be laws that strike against the conscience of the man who has to administer them. But it is a necessary presumption that all law, having the sanction of a body of lawmakers, is wiser than the individual. So one administers the bad laws with the good, feeling the shame and disgust that will eventually lead to change.

A magistrate is much more on his own than are the judges of the higher courts. He has no jury to help him decide guilt or innocence. Lawyers rarely appear for either side, so he must depend largely on his own knowledge of law and procedure, without the close check that able lawyers can offer. Accused people rarely make the best of their own defense; prosecuting officers are usually experienced and skillful. So it is often a magistrate's duty to bring out the defense by direct questions and by cross-examining prosecution witnesses. In the simplicity of rural courts a magistrate keeps his own full record of the evidence in longhand; apparently he may use a fountain pen, but I suspect that with a little effort one could dig up a law somewhere stipulating a goose quill. While doing all this, he must also keep control of his court, carefully follow the niceties of procedure, gauge the demeanor of witnesses, protect them from unfair cross-examination, ensure that inadmissible evidence is excluded. And then, having split his faculties in these various ways, he is left alone to reach his decision.

I think the loneliest moments of my life have been at the conclusion of defense and prosecution arguments in a closely contested case. Writing books is lonely work in that one must search one's mind alone, produce from it alone, make innumerable decisions alone; but nothing is irrevocable until the galley proofs are corrected, and one can always ask another human's opinion or advice. On the bench one is utterly alone and no one may help; at times things that do help must be disregarded. The decision will be irrevocable and it will directly affect another man's life in an important way. Time presses a little; one can adjourn to think things over if necessary, but to do so is an abuse if one merely seeks to defer the agony of decision. At such times I feel my frailty in fullest measure; emotion and prejudice intrude, mood is a danger, the very quickness of the brain in understanding both sides, the facility of words to express either decision, are hazards. The dignity of the court is a hazard, every facet of one's own humanity is a hazard.

The only refuge is in humility, an utterly convinced, completely self-effacing humility before the complexity of truth and the even greater complexity of human nature, in the solemn certainty that complete impartiality and complete honesty are beyond the power of man, no matter how he may strain for them. In this there is a measure of help towards the proper balance of head and heart and law that yields a fair decision.

COUNTRY MAGISTRATE
Out of Court

MY USUAL COURT DAYS ARE Monday and Saturday of each week, and so far as possible all cases are channeled to one or other of those two days. But a magistrate cannot order his affairs so simply as that; he is likely to be called upon at almost any hour of day or night, by anyone from an amiable drunk or a beaten wife to a policeman needing a warrant or a young girl running away from home.

One does not encourage these interruptions, but I think it is clear that a magistrate has an obligation to be reasonably accessible to the public. This stems primarily from the fact that if he is accessible he can be useful, but it is also implicit in every official failure, from the time of the first shaman in the first official cave, to be accessible. It is far too easy for an official who has a ponderous feeling for the dignity of his office to keep people away when they have real need of him. On the whole, people do not take advantage of accessibility; rather they tend to respect it and treat it courteously.

Most out-of-court work grows from family relationships—errant sons and daughters, irresponsible husbands and wives and fathers and mothers. Most of these affairs start in court, as juvenile cases, assault cases, or maintenance cases. Some go on for years, quiescent for months at a time, then suddenly in crisis that threatens to bring them to court again or break the family beyond repair.

The chance of any straightforward success in such cases is very small. Marriage is never an easy relationship and by the time the differences between two people have reached the stage that brings them to court, or even to a magistrate out of court, the real origins of the trouble have long been lost in incidental frictions and are almost impossible to uncover. But some sort of temporary patchwork to hold a family together is often possible, especially when children are involved; and when children are involved, every day that a family can be held together in some sort of unity is of value. Sometimes the patchwork, or renewals of it, hold until the children leave school and go out on their own. Then, with the pressure and urgency of the children removed, man and wife often find they can get along quite comfortably.

Though most of this work is unofficial, with only a vague shadow of some inadequate law held in the background, it is probably the most valuable work a magistrate ever does. Broken homes and poor citizenship tend to be self-perpetuating; most people who fail to make something good out of marriage are children of parents who failed in the same way. A broken home does not necessarily produce crime or criminals, but nearly all criminals within my experience have come from broken or inadequate homes. So the little pressures one can apply and the stumbling advice one offers are directed towards something much bigger than most courtroom sentences and admonitions.

So far as I know, Elkhorn has no more than the standard number of family problems, but I usually have two or three cases in the acute stage at any given time, and perhaps another half dozen that are threateningly dormant. On the whole the cases starting with assaults are the most likely to turn out well, perhaps because genuine and lively emotions are at work and can be played upon. The man is usually a little ashamed, the woman a little shaken by her audacity in bringing the thing out into the open, often pathetically sorry for the position in which she has put her man. The mere fact of remembering and recounting, in a calm, objective atmosphere, things that were said and done while the stove was hot, the children squawled, and a peg or two of liquor heated the blood, has a therapeutic value. Melodramatics are nearly always funny when described by amateurs.

Maintenance and nonsupport cases are tougher. The thing has usually dragged on much longer before coming to this stage, feelings are too often cold and deadly. But there are still strong arguments to be put forward: it is easy to show that the children will be better with two parents than one and that a man's earnings will do more to look after a family living together than one that is broken into two households. If there is any remnant of the mutual attraction that brought the two together in the first place, if there is any feeling for the bond of the years they have lived together and the children they have begun to raise together, something may be saved.

I think I worked harder and longer to hold Tom and Jane together than any other couple I have had to deal with. They had several children, a secure place in the community, a fine house carefully built by Tom and skillfully furnished by Jane, genuine affection for each other, everything necessary to a good life except the ability to understand each other and trust each other. It is more than eight years now since Jane laid the first assault charge, and for at least six of these years there were recurrent crises, each one of which threatened to break things up for good. Tom had an enormous and dangerous pride that made him try to hold Jane under rigid discipline; Jane loved a good time and had just the right mixture of irresponsibility and determination to insist upon having it from time to time.

After the first session in court, Jane and Tom usually came along to argue out their differences informally whenever the strain grew too great. Again and again I sat as referee, mostly listening, putting in occasional guiding words when I wasn't too confused myself, and again and again they settled things between them and went off to live in peace for another spell. But there came a time at last when it seemed that nothing would save the day.

I grew impatient. "You can't break up five children," I said, "and fifteen years of married life just because you're too obstinate to work things out between you. Being married is more important than that."

They looked at each other for a moment. "We aren't married," Jane said. "He won't marry me."

"I can't," Tom said. "I was married before and I don't know where my first wife is."

"You never tried to find her. You'd rather keep it this way so you can kick me out any time."

They argued it out from there and in the end Tom agreed to make a real effort to find the first wife and arrange for a divorce. I don't know whether he made it or not. They have moved to the Mainland now and I haven't seen them for some while; but they are still together.

May

There is never anything approaching a pattern in family cases, and I think that is why the law is so ineffective in dealing with them. Divorce is a heartless affair, morally and financially far removed from the lives of ordinary people. Lawyers enter into it, and cold law, and a synthetic religious restraint. Ordinary people are afraid of all these things. Divorce is evil because it is betrayal of an act of faith. It is legally serious because it is breach of an important civil contract. It is a problem to the state, because it leaves children improperly cared for. But it is essentially a matter between two people and I often think it might best be handled in the practical simplicity of a magistrate's court. The state's large issues might be occasionally slighted, but human issues would be given full values. As it is now, a magistrate deals with all the problems of divorce and a great many that the divorce courts disregard. He deals with them gropingly, guided by his knowledge of people and by such "wit, cunning and power" as he may have, backed only by the trust and respect people feel for his office. Perhaps this is the safest way. If the easy remedy of divorce were in his hands, he might not work so hard to find solutions within the bonds of matrimony.

At the opposite extreme of out-of-court work are the perennial minor offenders, the petty problem children of adult years who exist in every community. Jean was one, a French-Canadian veteran of the first war with a small pension for a wound, well on in years, illiterate, alone in the world except for intermittent drinking companions. So far as possible the police overlooked Jean's drinking bouts, chased him home to his shack when they had to, or kept him overnight in the lockup to sober up when it seemed unlikely he could make home. But occasionally their patience would wear out and Jean would appear in court. One day I threatened an interdiction order, to prevent him getting any liquor at all. He was up at my house that afternoon.

"Don't you put me on that list," he said.

"You can't drink yourself to death," I told him.

"Why not? Who's got a better right? It ain't much to ask from a country you fought for."

I couldn't find much to say to that, except that he'd have to keep from being a nuisance to people, including the police. Things went on as they always had for quite a while, but at last Jean was caught selling liquor to an Indian. So I made the order.

"Won't do any good," Jean said fiercely. "I'll get it."

"No, you won't," I said just as fiercely. "If any of your precious friends gives you a smell of liquor, he'll be in for three months."

Jean looked unhappy. "It's only a month to Christmas," he said.

I lifted the order in time for him to get his Christmas bottle. Three days later the police found him dead in his cabin. Not liquor, the doctor told me, just heart.

Interdiction orders aren't too effective because, as Jean pointed out, a bottle is usually procurable. But "the List" has an adverse social significance, and few of the problem children like to be on it. Prudence worries more about the List than any other penalty. She is a tall woman, normally handsome, good-natured and dignified. But in her cups she is easily provoked and when provoked she is devastating; her language is vivid, breakage piles swiftly about her, and even innocent bystanders sometimes get hurt. So Prudence—Overproof Prue, the disrespectful call her—is sometimes in trouble. When she is, especially when I have put her on the List, I can expect a long distance call from Winnipeg and it will be Prue's mother wanting news of her little daughter. A few days later Prue will come up to the house, wearing a handsome new outfit, her black hair gleaming like satin, her voice soft and lovely except for its faintest alcoholic rasp as she tries to talk herself off the List.

"No, Prue," I have to say, hating my unresponsive nature. "I said three months and that's what it is."

There are many others, simple warm-hearted inebriates whose serious ambitions have been drained away and whose moral standards have grown defective with misuse. They are never criminals, but they often slide into trouble that is close to crime. Not useful people, nor always ornamental, but kind, well-intentioned, and tolerant nearly always. In their good times they feel and express ideals far above anything they can live up to in their bad times, so it is hard to believe the inevitable chain of happenings will shortly bring them back to trouble again. Sometimes I think they waste other lives besides their own; sometimes I think they make other lives fuller because their frailties draw people into sacrifice and selfless effort that would not otherwise be made.

I suppose any free man must feel irritated by and contemptuous of the pettiness of much law. All law is basically an insult to human nature, often a deserved and necessary insult, but no less an insult for that. Law and government should be simply a convenience to enable people to live in groups without upsetting each other too much, but politicians and lawyers have developed both to the point where they affect every known activity. Perhaps the complexity of modern civilization is to blame, but I don't think petty, restrictive legislation is any solution. It simply sets a premium on cheating. "Manners," Burke said, "are of more importance than laws. The law touches us but here and there and now and then." When law tries to cover too much, anything it does not cover becomes, by inference, moral. Which is absurd.

The people of Elkhorn don't like the British Columbia liquor laws. They see nothing immoral in buying a bottle of whisky after 6:00 P.M. or on Sundays, so there is always a successful bootlegger or two in town, as there is in most British Columbia communities. The people don't like the bootleggers because they gouge too much money out of them and become fat and prosperous and boastful; they like to suggest they have influence in high places and are immune to prosecution. The plain truth is they are very hard to catch because no citizen will lay formal complaint or give evidence in court against them.

I don't like bootleggers because the fact that they are difficult to catch undermines people's respect for law in much more important matters; so I was delighted when an indignant correspondence started in the Elkhorn *Bugle* shortly after the war, directed against the bootleggers and their apparent immunity. I watched the correspondence closely and found the many names signed to it did not at all add up to a temperance group; rather they were the names of good-natured, easy-going people, in love with life and the good things of life. Here, I felt, was the ideal level from which to put things right.

Finally I invited all the names to come along one night and talk things over. They all came. It took a little while to get the point, but I got it in the end. Beer was still in short supply. The objection was not that bootleggers were bootlegging, but that they were handling so much of the limited supply of beer that there was not enough to keep the beer parlors open. This was a simple matter to put right, but it left the bootleggers still secure, if in temporarily short supply of one item.

May

Irritations like bootleggers grow out of petty restrictions that have no real moral base. Their indirect effect of fostering a contempt for law is far more serious than any direct offense they commit. There are literally thousands of restrictions on the statute books, passed by municipalities and provinces and in the fuzzier acts of the Dominion parliament itself, that the ordinary man has never heard of and never will hear of, though he may break many of them. Some of them conflict so sharply with superior legislation that they are never invoked, yet they remain on the books. Compared with this undistinguished clutter, the Criminal Code is nearly always hard and sharp and clear. There can be weariness of argument in hearing a case under it, repetition of evidence, confusion of technicalities, but most of its issues are genuinely based on injury or threat of injury to person or property. Its guiding morality is clear and clearly understood, for it is simply the statement of the civilization's own slowly developed morality.

When I first became a magistrate, I supposed I should find law dull. I am still layman enough to feel that much law is unnecessarily confusing, and to grow impatient with the turnings and twistings of lawyers who try to keep truth from finding its way out. Yet a court hearing requires such concentration from a magistrate that it is almost impossible for it to be dull. There is always a fascinating variation between witnesses, even truthful witnesses to the same event. There is the steady tension of trying to judge between truth and falsehood, between deliberate falsehood, falsehood combined with rationalization, and plain misconception; the added tension of regard for procedure; and always the astonishing background, seldom more than partially revealed, of emotion and behavior and character that led up to the crime that brought the case to court.

Even reading law is not dull, though again I had supposed it would be. I have spent many hours reading law in the past ten years and have found a sharp sense of spiritual experience in its deep humanity, its determination to block persecution or unfairness by rigid and faithful application of great principles to small matters. In this I have felt for myself the secure yet flexible base of democracy. In page after page of the well-annotated volumes I have found examination and assessment of human nature, based on slow experience, that come close to anticipating every distortion or perversion or misapprehension of truth. The law guards against emotional bias and careless thinking with a purity of intent that reaches the highest levels of human endeavor. Because it seeks a perfect balance between the protection of innocence and the punishment of guilt, it is full of imperfections. But it is built of collected wisdom, tried and re-tried by humane and brilliant minds to the end that a minimum of human frailty shall enter into judgment. And pervading this practical magnificence is a spiritual devotion to the idea that the worth of one man, any one man, transcends all practical considerations.

I have been warned that a magistrate inevitably makes enemies. If I have made any, I do not know them. There is criticism, of course, but less than I had expected and less, I think, than there should be. I sometimes hear the findings of the beer-parlor lawyers who gather on Saturday evenings to review my decisions over glasses set out on little round tables. They work on an emotional plane, without rules of evidence or procedure, and never assume less than supreme court powers. Quite often they reverse me, but I like to feel that they do so academically and objectively, exactly as would any superior court. The supporting arguments that are reported to me, usually based on background detail that did not and could not have come out in court, are always useful warning that nothing is so simple as it seems. Some of them have taught me to dig a little deeper than I might have into later cases.

In every form of expression, from the novels of Smollet to the cartoons of Capp, the country magistrate is a comic and slightly sinister figure. The public reckons him an occasional convenience, probably an old fool, more than likely crooked, certainly full of doddering prejudices. His knowledge of law, and usually his impartiality, are suspected by both defense and prosecuting attorneys. But the fact remains that a country magistrate deals with real people and real issues between them. He can do something to help the ordinary man's struggle with the complexities of law and something to put humanity into the robot nature of the state. In doing so he is forced to test and retest his own integrity, constantly learning how frail a creature he is. This seems to me a tough and challenging assignment. I can't imagine achieving perfection on the bench any more than I can imagine writing a perfect book, but there are similarities of demand in both jobs. It is no small thing to me to have learned that the offenses for which men are brought to judgment are not the strangely motivated, vicious things I had supposed. Only rarely can I not detect deep in myself some counterpart of the thoughts that produced a crime, and I do not always have to search so very far or very deep.

There is a famous picture by Georges Roualt called "Three Judges." I have read that it expresses evil—shallowness, avarice, cruelty, and unhealthy pride. Once I studied the picture for a long while trying to find all this. I remember the face of the center judge now; it seems to me the face of an anxious, worried man. Effort and concern are expressed there, and a feeling of personal inadequacy—not lack of intelligence or courage, but intense doubt of the man's own humanity, wisdom, power of understanding; and, above all, doubt of the mechanical means he must use to solve the human problem before him. I think I see in that man's face the whole jarring conflict between human compassion and the needs of a gregarious society. If so, I suspect he was a good judge.

JUNE

THE BIG SWALLOWTAIL BUTTER-
flies are most noticeable each year when the lilacs and the
scarlet hawthorn are out. They seem very strong and positive
creatures for butterflies, powerful in flight, their great black
and yellow wings carrying thick bodies easily over the treetops if necessary; and they are purposeful in feeding as their
black legs grip and crawl over the faces of the flowers and
their long black tongues reach in to suck the sweet fluids. I
look forward to their coming in June as I look forward to
my daughter Mary's birthday and the glory of the peonies in
the flower border and the droop and fragrance of the false
acacia flowers in the rain that always comes as their bloom is
fullest.

June on Vancouver Island is normally a fairly wet month,
wet enough to make the hay crop difficult to harvest and to
make one worry about the fate of the newly hatched blue
grouse and ruffed grouse. Yet its remembered days are the
most beautiful of all the year, with clean brilliance of sunlight and warmth, free from the heaviness of later summer

days. Mary's birthday, on the second, I remember as always fine, with a mass of adoring little girls running in bright dresses all over the lawn and Mary quiet and humble, unaware of the adoration or of her own quiet loveliness that inspires it. She was eleven this year, very conscious of her day, as all the children are; and I wonder, without asking her, if she expects always to see on that day the swallowtails hanging on the lilac clusters and fluttering in almost perpendicular display flights from the grey gravel of the driveway. Perhaps something else than this has caught her mind and will be remembered as an expected part of the year's tribute to her. If so I hope it has all the strength and beauty and grace of the great swallowtails and all their associations with the garden loveliness of June.

For June surely is the flower gardener's month. My small border is rich then with irises and columbine and lupins and violas. And over and among them all the peonies, growing with a fine freedom and blooming with a magnificence that no gardener of my careless habits and feeble skill has any right to expect. What have I ever done for them? A deep, sandy loam is here, reinforced at the time of planting several years ago. I weed a little and put on an annual mulch of peat moss; I scatter sulphur about the crowns of the plants in early spring if I remember to and stake and tie the foliage during May. That is all, yet they are the true glory of the border year after year, professional in their size and splendor, brilliant in every shade from deepest red to palest pink and cream and white. Only the cautious growth of the delphiniums behind them reminds me that my reflected glory will not outlast their honest performance.

The birds of the garden in June are the warblers, the yellow warblers and the Audubon warblers above all. I write this now as if I had known and felt it all my life, yet even ten years ago I should not have written it. Warblers are not showy

birds or noisy birds or very bold birds, but they are, in woodland countries, very numerous birds. Once one has become
conscious of warblers they seem to be everywhere. Some time
in June of each year there is a large-scale garden function at
our house and I usually go for a walk up the river on that
afternoon. I am always amazed at the numbers of yellow
warblers I find, nesting or singing from the tops of high willow trees, darting out to catch flies or carrying a full catch
back to the nest. They are such beautiful birds to be common,
so brightly and completely yellow. I feel this even at a distance from them, but when I am close enough to see the faint
red streaks on the male's yellow breast, my mind denies everything I know and calls them rare and strange and beautiful
beyond any common experience.

The Audubon warbler is still more beautiful. The first one
I ever saw was hunting flies along the eaves trough of the
house, brilliant in black and yellow and grey and white, darting out at times and hovering like a flycatcher, battering the
larger flies down to the ground where he could master and
grip them more easily. From time to time he would fly away
behind the house and I knew there must be a nest there somewhere. I found it next day, high up in one of the acacia trees,
and watched for a while. The parents were feeding the young
birds steadily, returning normally at six-minute intervals,
though difficulty of some kind occasionally broke the rhythm
with a gap of ten or twelve minutes; when that happened
there was the quick recompense of a two-minute return. They
were still working at nine o'clock at night.

One summer they nested in a tree branch within five or six
feet of the roof, and that was the summer we reroofed the
house, with carpenters working day after day. It was also the
summer of our big earthquake, when the house shook as
though every stud would break, chimneys clattered down for

fifty miles around, and the tops fell out of the mountains all through the heart of the Island. But the Audubon warblers raised their brood and they have been back faithfully ever since then, to nest in the main orchard or out along the driveway in the balsams.

A tree lover should, I suppose, disapprove of the sapsuckers and I admit that I feel most at ease in my admiration when I see them well up the river in May, around the Island Pools, as I fish for the small steelhead run. They sweep clear across the breadth of the river in high swooping flight and the spring sunlight catches the crimson of head and neck and breast and the yellow of the lower belly until one disbelieves a little the brilliance one has seen. Then the bird sweeps back and the brilliance is brighter than before, yet an acceptable part of all the magnificence of the place—one with the bold flight of the pileated woodpeckers and the bandtail pigeons as they cross on the same line, with the mergansers and water ousels, with the leap of the white water and the lift of the tall firs and maples along the banks.

Four or five years ago the sapsuckers made a brutal attack on the Golden Grimes tree; three or four years ago they circled the main trunk of the walnut; for the last two or three years they have worked busily each June on the rowan trees in the driveway. The marks that bored right down to sapwood on the Grimes and the walnut are only slight pits in the bark now and neither tree seems harmed.

Watching them last year on the rowans I could hardly believe that the limbs they attacked would survive. The birds were extremely tame, announcing themselves with sharp woodpecker cries until I came out of the house to watch. It was easy enough to walk right up under the trees without disturbing them and to watch the work for minutes at a stretch from five or six feet away. Their sharp and skillful beaks cut the bark in even rectangles, a quarter-inch wide by something less than half an inch long. Between the rectangles were untouched strips of bark perhaps an eighth of an inch wide, and the pattern would be repeated right around the branch, then repeated again above and below until a six- or eight-inch length of the branch looked like a honeycomb.

It was easy work for the sapsuckers. They drove their bills fast when they worked, but rested often, screaming in triumph, cocking their vivid heads on one side to take a bright-eyed look at me or at the latest rectangle, occasionally scooping the sides of their beaks along the gleaming run of sap or darting a swift and certain stroke at an insect that had been drawn to the feast.

I think the trees can stand them. At least the birds are wise enough to vary their attack from year to year, taking a rich crop, then leaving the tree to build a new abundance. They could, I suppose, become too numerous, but so far some creature or condition seems to have them under good control. If that should fail, I suppose I'd have to take serious thought. It's hard to know whether it would be cheaper to plant new trees or go out and rattle tin cans.

ORGANIZATIONS

IN A SMALL RURAL COMMUNITY only a complete recluse can escape taking active part in some form of local government. Ann and I are both reluctant joiners and I personally am socially lazy, at least in more concrete issues. In spite of this, and in spite of steadily increasing skill in avoiding casual commitments as well as the more formal cares of office, we have both been measurably involved in local affairs throughout fifteen years of married life.

We arrived in Elkhorn Village immediately after a provincial election in which the Liberals had handsomely defeated the Conservatives. Local interest in the election was fairly strong, chiefly because it was supposed that the patronage system would promptly change the holder of every government job and privilege—a matter of no small importance in the early thirties, in a settlement where most jobs depended on the government or the good will of the large logging companies.

I had heard much of the workings of the patronage system in British Columbia, but had never seen it at first hand and had not been able to believe that it would actually concern itself with the tiny detail and the pathetically underpaid jobs it was supposed to. I now saw it fire a Conservative road foreman and his crew and hire a full set of Liberals. This, the wise ones said, was only a start; the liquor vendor, the policeman, the game warden, the public-works inspector, probably even the coroner, the medical-health officer, the schoolteachers, and the local bootlegger would be replaced by more orthodox politicians. There was plenty of concern, much of it disinterested. Spontaneous indignation meetings formed up in the store and the garage, on the wharf, in farmhouses, on wood lots, at whist drives and dances, wherever people saw each other. None of the indignation seemed likely to reach any place where it would have an effect, so I concentrated it in a single angry letter, which was promptly subscribed by a string of indignant signatures and mailed to the newly elected member. In a little while he replied, mildly surprised, mildly hurt, mildly suggesting that things might not be nearly so bad as they seemed. We pursued the matter, a shade more temperately; but interest gradually faded, perhaps because there were no more job changes. Political habit had been followed to the disadvantage of the Conservative road crew—which, no doubt, had come into its tenure by the same way it went out—but I think the patronage system in these simpler and more obvious manifestations was already a dead issue. It probably had been for some while.

There were at that time in the settlement of Elkhorn only three really active organizations—a branch of the Canadian Legion, the Elkhorn Liberal Association, and the Elkhorn District Board of Trade. The Legion was specialized and limited. The Liberal Association was also limited and, as I have suggested, shamelessly out for its own; it was reputed to have a sinister power at high levels of government, but it seemed to achieve little if anything beyond this replacement of the road crew. Which left only the Board of Trade to speak for the affairs of three or four thousand people who lived in scattered unconcern over ten thousand square miles of woods and islands and inlets.

The Board had some twenty or thirty members, of whom less than ten usually managed to turn up at the monthly meetings. There was a nucleus of small businessmen, store and garage owners, hotel and resort men, but anyone was welcome at the meetings and the constitution readily stretched to permit anyone who wanted to join. Loggers, farmers, fishermen, mechanics, schoolteachers, doctors, carpenters, clerks, and plumbers were members, which made a sufficiently faithful cross section of the people who lived in the district. Dues were small and the Board's funds were never more than enough to meet the fixed obligations, which included a salary of twenty-five dollars for the secretary. Yet it worked. It considered and discussed to the best of its ability anything and everything that was brought before it. It refused to be overawed by the local influence and power of the big logging companies, and it spoke out boldly for any cause it believed in.

We met in the back room of a warehouse, by the light of a single unshaded bulb, in the friendly informality of first names and known qualities. We were none of us orators or politicians or expert in the ways of government; there was no room for insincerity or fancy performance. We simply tried to understand a problem, develop an opinion that seemed reasonable to all of us, then take whatever action seemed most likely to get results. Gradually we became quite skillful in working a brief or a resolution up and down through the proper government channels, in using the good will of the press, and enlisting the support of other organizations when these were affected.

We were not, in any real sense, local government. We had no positive responsibilities and no administrative powers. Unincorporated rural communities and districts are defined as "unorganized" and are administered directly by the provincial government in Victoria. We were simply the natural collective voice for an area whose residents could otherwise have spoken for themselves only individually. It often seemed to the most optimistic of us that we were achieving little, and that little very slowly. Yet now, looking back over the records of those easygoing meetings, I am amazed at how effective and how often right we were. We fought a gallant and unceasing fight for forest conservation and watershed protection; neither has yet been achieved in any real sense, but there has been a tremendous change in forest policy over the years. We examined possibilities of a local hospitalization plan and in doing so undoubtedly hastened the province-wide plan that is now in effect. We argued for scientific management of commercial and game fisheries with a persistence that I am sure did a good deal to obtain the present advances towards this. We fought for provincial parks and an authority to manage them—which we now have. We urged the opening of certain agricultural land to settlers; it has since been opened and now supports some of the steadiest settlers in the district. We argued and fought for improved roads, bridges, wharves, mail and transportation services, all of which have since come. We expressed opinions on such national matters as old-age pensions and social assistance and unemployment insurance. We took the initiative in such local matters as the purchase and management of an ambulance, the development of a fire department, the improvement of sanitation.

Obviously none but the most local of these things was achieved by the small, quiet meetings of the Board. But the clear progress that has been made towards the larger objectives is evidence enough that the unorthodox debates and the halting opinions were essentially sound. When John Tollance, first generation from Yorkshire, huge and slow, heaved to his feet and said that farm settlers were soundest of all, he was right. When Ian McAllister, from Scotland by way of the prairies, said sharply it was wickedness to burn the woods behind the logging, he was echoed by Women's Institutes and Sewing Circles, by church guilds and trade unions across the province; and the government knew they were right. So it was when Ivar Nelson, late of Norway, spoke for the fishermen, when Ned Harris, Sussex-born hotel man, spoke for the parks, when the Danes spoke and the Swedes and Finns and Italians and native Canadians, each for the thing that touched his imagination and reached his heart. Central governments, reaching greedily across an empty continent, had left large sections of people with no ready way to speak for themselves. So the little organizations moved in and became the spiritual descendants of the wapentake, the parish council and the town meeting.

Long before we had a child of school age, and again in spite of our better intentions, Ann and I were drawn into the affairs of the School Board. Rural school boards do important business, but no one pays them attention or gratitude until things go wrong. In this case the district had developed a strong economy faction, aggressively supported by many property owners who had no children or whose children were grown beyond school age. Parents and potential parents were just as strong numerically, but had not been paying very close attention. Then the matter of adding a new room to the school came up. The need was unquestionable—every existing room was crowded beyond the possibility of adding a single desk—but the cost was to be five thousand dollars and the economy faction would have none of it. The leader of the economy group was Evan Langton, a tall, spare, hawk-nosed farmer, dark eyed and intense, a bachelor, a man of fair education—some said he had studied to be a doctor—and a man who had expected better things for himself. He was not essentially a bitter man, nor unkindly, but he yearned for leadership and at some time he had probably yearned for a wife and family. He had become a drinking man and he found a measure of leadership among a number of small stump ranchers, bachelors, loggers and Scandinavians for the most part, who were also drinking men.

Evan had property in the settlement besides his farm, so he had influence and friendship with the more important property owners as well as with the bachelor stump ranchers. But to make quite sure of a voting majority he had taken to priming a dozen or so of the stump ranchers with overproof rum and bringing them along to the annual School Board meetings. It was this that roused the parents and prospective parents, including ourselves. An unheard-of total of seventy or eighty voters crowded into the small schoolroom for the meeting and somehow I found myself in the chair.

From the chair the meeting looked formidable, and there was about it a tense, uneasy hush quite unlike the cheerful ease of most village meetings. Evan sat silent and dark at a desk in the front row and behind him was ranged his solid voting bloc, big, heavy-shouldered men for the most part, dressed in their town clothes, ill at ease, but breathing fumes of determination mixed with the sterner stuff that Evan had used to rally them.

The business of the meeting started easily. Ann was nominated as a trustee and elected without difficulty when Evan unexpectedly seconded her nomination. It was a gesture of chivalry, yet also one of contempt; the addition of the new room was a matter for the meeting, not the trustees. And he was sure of the meeting.

The election of an auditor for the year was another matter. The progressives nominated Ted Hale, the town's ablest bookkeeper and the auditor of the previous year. Then one of Evan's big Vikings pushed himself up from the tiny desk he was sharing with a friend of equal size. He spoke eloquently and to the point:

"Ay t'ank we better have some change. Some people together all the time, nobody knows what happens. Ay lak to see for Mr. Sam Harper here to be auditor."

I felt little Jamie Black, the secretary-treasurer, move sharply beside me. "If that lame-brain Sassenach is going to see in my books," he said, "ye'll have my resignation." Sandy-haired and quick-tempered, sharp and spare with a dollar when it was right to be, Jamie had been the School Board's working brain and soul for years. But the nominations were fair and I knew there was nothing to be done to help him. Evan's man got in by two votes. Jamie expressed his feelings by sweeping a mass of papers to the floor and muttering grimly as he bent to pick them up.

The meeting was still strained, but not unhappy. People liked Jamie and knew he was doing a good job, but most of them had felt his sharp and autocratic impatience at one time or another and even the progressives were not sorry to see him get a minor setback. Besides, the fight has been orderly so far, good clean fun that anyone could mix in with a clear conscience. Evan's bloc sat in solemn dignity, perspiring a little in the hot evening sunlight that played through the room, entirely without the alcoholic belligerence rumor had threatened.

Jamie began to read the annual statement. An item was challenged, a voucher demanded. Disdainfully, Jamie produced it. Another item was challenged, then another and another. A voucher was missing and Jamie had to send down the road to his house for it, while the meeting waited. Jamie's neck was flushed, then his face and forehead reddened clear up under the thinning sandy hair. Finally he slammed his papers down on the desk. "I'll no stand for it," he said. "The books is good. That's more than can be said for the standing of some of them that's talking here tonight. There's a mint of taxes unpaid around this town."

He looked straight at Evan as he spoke and Evan got slowly to his feet. "Would you be insinuating my taxes isn't paid, Mr. Black?" he asked softly.

"I'd as soon see the receipts," Jamie said contemptuously.

Evan looked at me. "Is that necessary, Mr. Chairman?" I nodded. He handed me a paper and I passed it to Jamie. Jamie studied it.

"So ye went down and paid this morning," he said at last.

"It's all that's needed," Evan said, and I noticed that he was swaying a little on his feet. "I've witnesses here, all about the room, and I'll be suing for defamation of character, Mr. Black." He glanced at me. "You'll hear from my lawyers, too, Mr. Chairman. There's . . ."

"Fine," I said hastily. "Fine. But there'll be a place to go into all that. Let's get on with the school business now."

The meeting sighed. It seemed to know the big moment had come and gone and it was right. Evan kept the fight alive. He moved that the meeting should not hear the school principal on the need for the new room and was narrowly defeated. Two nullifying amendments to the main motion were moved and defeated. The main motion itself came up and I ordered a sealed vote. Tension held until the scrutineers had made their last check. A majority of eight gave the trustees power to borrow five thousand dollars and build the addition. There were some that had not earned their rum ration and then, too, Evan may have miscalculated in other ways; almost any big Scandinavian bachelor is a pushover for anything that will "do some good for the kiddies."

Less than a dozen years later, quietly and almost without opposition, Elkhorn District voted half a million dollars to build a whole new school on a new and better site. There was a hundred per cent poll in the area up around Evan Langton's farm, and no dissenting vote.

There is an incorporated village of Elkhorn now, with city fathers, local taxes, local bylaws, and all the rest. Board of Trade meetings have an attendance of thirty or forty members. There is a ratepayer's organization, Rotary and Kinsmen's Clubs flourish, the Liberal Association has revived under new management; a full-fledged Rod and Gun Club has taken over the functions of one of the old Board of Trade committees, and a strong P.T.A. keeps parents interested in the school. These are only a few of the organizations; at least a dozen others do business and every one of them seems to have a woman's auxiliary that is just a little busier than the parent body.

Ann and I remain reluctant joiners and are helped a little in this by the fact that we live outside the village. Since we have three children in school and another growing up to it, Ann is, for the second time in four years, president of the P.T.A. It sounds very logical until, as Ann says, you stop to think that the most important business a mother of four can have is to stay home and mind her children in loving peace and calm.

For my part, since I write books about fish and game, I'm president of the Rod and Gun Club. Again, it seems very natural and logical until you stop to think that the most important business a writer can have is to stay home and write books. Going out, for either of us, means neglecting something, if not several things—children, garden, livestock, reading, correspondence, visitors, or even a simple chance to walk around the place and enjoy it. When we do have to go we complain bitterly to each other and describe the measure of our stupidity with a beautiful precision.

It is very easy to be offhand or even severely critical of this multiplicity of organizations. They do waste time, they do duplicate and sometimes stultify each other's efforts, they are an easy fulfillment for people who would be better employed in finding more difficult fulfillment in their own lives. Many of them, with nationwide affiliations, function far too often as pressure groups, almost as evil and out of place in a democracy as the lobbies of big business. Yet they have one supreme function, often disregarded in the press of business with which they crowd themselves; they give people a chance to meet each other and know each other and like each other. Ann comes back from a P.T.A. meeting and I look up smugly from the desk and ask, "How was it?"

"Just the usual stuff," she says wearily. Then her face is suddenly full of life. "But you should have *seen* those Grade Three children in their little act. Golly, they were cute. And that little Mrs. Chaudiere, straight out from Quebec, the nicest kind of person. And Molly Hanson's husband's got a new job and they're moving. I'm certainly glad for her. Joan Heffley's looking after the Meaker children while their mother goes into the hospital—that's a wonderful woman; I wish I could do half what she does. Jane Harris, the stinker, says . . . "

And when I come back from a Rod and Gun meeting I answer the same question in much the same way. "Same old stuff. Kind of nice though. We got through a lot of business, but it's more like a bull session than a formal meeting. Everybody's talking hunting and fishing and why animals do this or that, and everybody interested. You have to check them once in a while or they'd never get anything done. That guy Jake's a real conservationist—talks good sense and really means it. And old Norm was going just as well as ever. It's a nice club. Nobody ever fights very seriously."

The truth of it is, I suppose, that we're neither of us as anti-social as we'd like to think and we'll probably go on neglecting more important things for the warmth there is in a roomful of people learning to know one another.

JULY

We found the cedar wax-
wings nesting first in a tall native spirea on the river bank just
above the swimming place. That was years ago and probably
they were nesting nearby for many years before that. Wax-
wings are the sleekest, proudest and best groomed of all the
little birds I know and they let one get close enough to admire every last detail of their perfection. The high, sharp
crest and the smooth chestnut of breast and head are easy to
see and identify; the handsome yellow band at the tip of the
grey tail is a little more difficult, but still easy enough; and
one must be very close and in just the right position to see the
tiny patch of sealing wax scarlet on the tips of the wing
feathers, but the birds are generous enough to show even this
quite often.

Waxwing families built nests in the spirea for several years
after we first found them there and others, perhaps descendants of the original birds, built in the nearby trees of the main
orchard. I watched for them anxiously in 1946 but there was
no nest in the spirea and I was almost afraid they had found

some more attractive place to raise their families. Then, on the last day of June, I heard their sharp little tzee-note in an elder bush and saw a pair playing like lovebirds. Their nest was already built in the Grimes tree, with four purple-splotched eggs on the lining of black sheep's wool. They hatched safely, as did another nest two apple trees away.

This year there was a nest in the Gravenstein and another in one of the Yellow Transparents. I found the first as I was watching the hair nest of a chipping sparrow just above it and still don't know how I had missed it before, because the female was sitting tight already, with her grey tail angled sharply upwards. The nest in the Transparent tree was in the lowest branches, trailing sheep's wool, and many times I watched from within four or five feet, admiring the sharp black beak and the clear black line across the bird's head, carefully avoiding her frightened eye in the hope she would think I did not see her. Again the young birds hatched and flew from both nests; in late September, just before they leave, we shall see them feeding on the rowan berries.

A much shyer, or perhaps merely wilder, bird of July is the western tanager. I watch for them eagerly because no other bird we have is so brilliantly colored and summer would not seem summer if I had not seen one. This year I saw them first in the old orchard, a male in his finest plumage, scarlet head, yellow-gold body, black wings, his green and yellow female with him. It was a fine enough thing to see, but one year we saw them first on the limbs of a big balsam tree with all their brilliance set out against the velvet green of the dark foliage.

July is highest and hottest summer, the time of road dust and forest fires, of warm evenings when the nighthawks and swallows fly high and the whole earth and the air above it seems to hum with movement and completion. It is almost impossible to look at any square foot of ground without seeing movement and strife, birth and life and death; and for every visible movement a hundred are hidden under rocks and roots and in the depths of the soil itself. Move a stone and there will be a nest of small black ants under it. They hurry in fright to tug at their big, dirty-yellow eggs and the few pale grubs already hatched. An earthworm moves and is attacked at once; it thrashes about, turns quite pale, twitches for a moment or two longer, then seems dead, all within the space of a minute. A black beetle tries to scramble across the nest, is attacked and flipped over, rights himself and manages to drag away with two or three ants still clinging to him. Wood lice cross slowly and cautiously, feeling ahead of them and clinging to grass stalks. The moment a feeler touches an ant, the louse stops and freezes. These are not attacked.

For several minutes after the stone is moved the whole scene is catastrophe, confusion, and panic. There seems no coherence in the efforts of the ants to move the eggs and they seem to be achieving nothing at all. Half an hour later there will not be an ant or an egg to be seen and the whole nest will be smoothly rearranged under another stone or log nearby.

The mathematical precision and efficiency of colony creatures such as ants and termites and bees and wasps repel me and frighten me as does nothing else in nature. Such creatures are nearly always fierce and aggressive—honey bees and termites are exceptions to this, I suppose—but they are also subservient and stupid. I know that this is their mode of survival, I know that the intricacies of it have fascinated better minds than mine, and I can feel the fascination myself as I watch a hornet hunting flies or ants swarming up a tree trunk, or when I check the progressive growth of the grubs across the open layers of a wasp's nest. I regret destroying a wasp's nest or a colony of ants when, as often happens, I must. Yet I cannot like them or feel an affinity with them as I can with most creatures, and the sense of revulsion persists, as senseless as the revulsion that so many men feel for snakes.

I think that all creatures move more freely in the warm calm of midsummer and this is especially true of the long late evenings between seven or eight o'clock and darkness. I think of a cougar coming out of the timber onto a railroad grade, serenely careless of my nearness as he started to his night of hunting. I think of young raccoons playing around the salal-shielded base of a big tree, of beaver swimming quietly in their ponds or in the broader streams where they live in the banks; I remember grouse coming out along dusty roads and deer stepping silently into swamps and bears feeding carelessly on the hillsides. In spite of the hunting animals, there seems a loosening of tension in those summer evenings, as though the growth of young creatures made all creatures bolder and the rich plenty of summer feed overbalanced the need for caution and suspicion.

I remember a July walk of a few summers ago for all these reasons and also for the series of shrinking time factors that largely controlled it. I had flown into a lake in the heart of Vancouver Island a few days earlier, meaning to fly out again on Saturday afternoon to be in good time for Mary's First Communion at nine-thirty on Sunday morning. Saturday was a day of rainstorms and low clouds that closed in the valleys and made flying among the mountains impossible. Because there seemed hope that the weather might change and because half an hour's flight is so much simpler than a fifteen- or twenty-mile walk, I waited too long. But at eight o'clock in the evening I started to walk the abandoned logging grade that led out from the foot of the lake.

The first time factor pressed from the start. I had not been over the way I was traveling before, but I knew that it meant fording the Elk River where the trestles had been washed out and I knew that the river was high. I wanted to get there before dark. I was also mildly curious about my own physical condition, because I had not walked five miles at a stretch since my discharge from a military hospital over a year before. It was raining hard and I began to walk fast.

Almost at once I noticed a cougar scrape in the grade, then bear droppings full of deer hair, then another cougar scrape. It was quiet in spite of the rain, and it was the time of movement, so I began to watch closely in the hope of seeing the cougar. I saw only deer. First a doe and two fawns near a little lake. Then a single young buck, his horns in the velvet, then another doe, then a group of twelve deer up on the hillside above me. I began to count them.

Three or four miles from the big lake I saw a black bear at the edge of a swamp, less than a hundred feet from the grade. I stopped to watch him as he walked the logs and reared up to reach the salmonberries, watched too long and hurried on. I counted more deer, once a band of thirty on the steep side of a draw above me, brought the count to a hundred, then lost track. I forced through the wetness of alders growing thickly along the grade, came out of them and still judged myself far from the crossing of the Elk. I began to walk faster, sometimes running for short distances on the down grades. In a cut I saw another bear only thirty or forty feet from the grade and angling up towards it. I hurried to be ahead of him and made it so narrowly that he fell backwards at seeing me and rolled over twice before he could gather his legs under him and make off the way he had come.

There was still daylight when I came to the river and judged I could make the crossing without swimming. The water was fast and cold and the gravel underfoot was loose and yielding. There was a deep place near the far bank, but there was also a cedar root I could grab, so I made it upright and swung myself out of the water.

My next time factor was to reach the lodge on the lower lake before everyone was in bed. I had come five or six miles out of a total of twelve and I thought I might make the lodge by eleven o'clock or soon after. I ran steadily through the remaining daylight, came to the steel of the main line, and hurried on. Soon it was dark and I had to watch for the open ties of the trestles. I found them safely by listening for the run of creeks off the hillside, but it slowed me and I missed the turning to the lodge in the darkness. By the time I knew I had missed it I could see a light in Walter's place across the foot of the lake and made up my mind to go on to that.

There were new time factors now. It would be midnight before I could get to Walter's, picking my footing across the log trestle at the foot of the lake and finding my way up from it to the road. From Walter's it was still twenty miles to Elkhorn and there might or might not be a car available. I arrived and got poor Walter out of bed and found there was no car.

"I'll go on to Jim's," I said. At least it was road, no trestles to worry about.

"That's thirteen miles," Walter said. "You've walked far enough. Better get some sleep now and phone for a taxi from one of the logging camps tomorrow morning. Camp Ten is only six miles."

He cooked a supper for me, gave me a drink and an alarm clock and a bed in a cabin. At daylight I was on the road again, a little wet and a little stiff, but with a new and more urgent time factor to worry about. It seemed a foolproof affair. Five miles to the Camp Ten turning—six-thirty should make it easily. A taxi on its way by seven. Home at eight or eight-thirty, plenty of time to change and get to church. I took delight in the grey morning, in the cautious stirring of the grouse, in a deer that crossed the road ahead of me, in a splendid tanager perched boldly in a willow tree. At six-thirty I came to the turning. But it was two miles, not one, to the camp. And it took a while to get the phone working. At seven-thirty they told me the taxi was on its way. Old Dan Harluk, the rigger, came past along the track as I left the phone box.

"Where you going now?" he asked.

"I'll start walking and meet the cab," I said. "Might catch a little time that way."

"Stay here and wait. You can't catch time. Nobody can." He picked up a couple of straps, slung them across his shoulder, and went off, short-stepping on the ties as loggers do.

But my time factor was near danger point now, so I walked. I came to the turning and there was no taxi. I calculated again. Home by nine, barely time to change. I walked on, past the big swamp, past Squarehead Lake, spotting turning places so that there should be no delay when the taxi came. I saw more grouse and more deer, but no taxi, and the time factor closed in on me and I began to lose hope. A truck passed, going the wrong way, and a carload of fishermen. At eight-fifty, five miles from where I had phoned, I met my taxi. We drove straight to the church and at nine-thirty-two I was inside, watching the back of Mary's white veil in the front pew, still wearing Elk River water in my clothes.

CHILDREN

WHEN WE GOT MARRIED ANN
and I were not, we said, going to do anything so Edwardian
as raise a lot of children. It was 1934. We had no money
nor, to be quite realistic about it, the slightest prospect of getting any more than we needed to keep from starving. And we
had a great many things to do, none of which fitted in with
small children. And in any case it was not at all the sort of
world into which wise and conscientious parents should wish
to bring children.

So far as I can remember, I was quite serious about all this
at the time. Ann, I am sure, was not serious about it then or at
any other time. Within a couple of years we had Valerie Joan
lying on a blanket and staring at the ceiling while her mother
painted the walls in an upstairs room of the house we had
somehow bought. In two more years we had Mary Charlotte
and Ann was calling herself "The Great Earth Mother." So
Alan came, still before Pearl Harbor, and after Alan, with a
decent gap to allow for the last few years of the war, Celia.
That may not be an enormous family by Victorian or Edwardian standards, but it's enough to help the increasing world
population towards its third billion.

Today, which is in late July of 1949, has been hot and
sunny, with a slight haze of smoke from out in the islands,
and a westerly breeze stirring the full summer foliage of the
maples. The river is very low, spread so thinly over its wide
bed that rocks show where they hardly ever do and the big
bar up by the islands has only a few little runs of fast water

over it. So Valerie, Mary, Alan, and I took rods and reels and fly lines and flies and went up to fish for trout. Celia, who is not quite two, stayed at home, as did her mother, who was glad to have an empty house and a fair chance to get things done for a day.

I thought I was going fishing with children, that they would dabble around for a little while, then find something else more amusing to do. But that wasn't the way of it at all. They went off along the shallow water of the bar, quite independently of me, far up until they felt they could all arrange themselves in good places, then began to fish very seriously. I decided to let the first surges of excitement die down before I tried to give any help, but when I went up an hour or so later they were still full of enthusiasm and concentration. One good trout was in the bag. Several others, just under the legal eight-inch length, had been turned back—a little regretfully, but without hesitation. They took time out to tell me about it, then went back to their business. I watched for a little while, then threw a fly out and hooked a fair-sized fish. Everyone went on fishing except Alan, who came down and netted the fish for me, then took it back to show his sisters. I threw again and hooked another fish, rather better than the first one. That seemed to persuade them I had found a good place, because I was almost immediately crowded out by three very determined fishermen and there was nothing to do but move off and catch another fish a little farther up.

At three o'clock or thereabouts Mary said she was hungry.

"Want to go home and get something to eat?" I asked.

"What would you do if we weren't here?"

"Go on up and try the canyon," I said.

"Then we'll go too," they all said. "We're not going home till you do."

At the canyon they quickly picked out places they liked,

waded out, and went to work. I moved on up to fish some fast runs, picked up a nice fish, and found Valerie cheerfully beside me, ready to take over. It was nine o'clock and almost dusk when we got home, and no one had said anything more about being hungry. There wasn't the slightest need to say anything about being tired, because they weren't tired.

I have written rather fully of this because it is fresh in my mind and because it seems to say what I want to say about children. Not that they go fishing, but that they are suddenly and unexpectedly independent and competent little creatures, developed beyond the recognizable cause and effect of day-to-day influences, not mere pale reflections of what they have been taught or shown. There was Valerie, the athlete of us all, tall and slender and strong, wading in hip boots with ease and laughter where many boys of her age would hesitate to go, casting far less well than she knows how, breaking off flies, caring little about anything except being out where she was. And Mary, who is sometimes easily tired and discouraged, standing beside me in the last end of the evening, more determined than any of us to catch one more fish. I was working a big fish I had risen twice before, earlier in the day, and rose him again almost at once but still did not touch him. After that I gave him the fly from every possible angle, drifted, dragged, jumped, even drowned, and could not move him. I had thought Mary engrossed in her own fishing, but afterwards, as we went homewards along the bar, she said, "Daddy, you were teasing that fish every way you could."

And Alan, whose muscles are not yet really strong enough to handle a fly rod, perched on a rock with the landing net. Little boy in the summer, I thought, watching the ripples on the water all about him and the dense screen of the leaves on the trees behind him. But he was more than that, a creature of choice, putting a deliberate trust in me to hook a fish and make work for the net that he still finds the most exciting part of going fishing.

Having children may be one of the most natural of mankind's activities, but it is also the most presumptuous. What can one offer them in heredity, in upbringing, in health or attractiveness or adaptability or skill or wisdom or any of the factors that will tend to keep them safe from the deep and tormenting unhappinesses that can reach into human lives? Can one reasonably hope to feed them, clothe them, educate them, and give them scope to realize themselves? Ann and I decided that we could do at least as well on these points as most people who have children; and we also decided that as we ourselves were finding the world an exciting and challenging place, it was reasonable to suppose that our children would find it equally good. It all sounded then, as it sounds now, an admirably detached and unemotional approach to the problem. But I am quite sure that the decision was far more deeply based than this, that it grew out of needs in ourselves that were physical, emotional, and spiritual rather than merely intellectual.

As it is now, we know we were right. It would have been impossible for Ann not to have had children and, in a less compelling sense, impossible for me also. What is far more important, it would have been impossible for these children not to have been born. Not because they are unusually brilliant or unusually beautiful or exceptionally gifted—they may be any of these things or none of them—but because they are people, each one, even Celia at two, its own self, with its own driving essence, its own future, its own will and mold to shape that future. It is all very well to theorize about children before they are born. Once they are born they are fact, not theory.

As they grow and develop they become more and more plainly fact, sharper entities, more and more of themselves and in themselves. This, I believe, is the reason for parenthood and the true satisfaction of parenthood, that the child shall grow always outward from the parent, becoming strong in its own right, taking hold, passing beyond traceable experience and influence into individuality. It is nothing, ultimately, that the parent has produced it and worked for it and raised it. What matters is that a man or woman, capable of individual thought and emotion, shall go forth into the world.

Once when I was milking in the barn and Alan was standing beside me, he said, "Daddy, I know it can't happen, but when I grow up I want to have a farm here and write books and be the judge."

"Why can't it happen?" I asked above the sound of the milk in the pail.

"Because I want it to be this same place and I want the cow to be Primrose, and I want Kitty and Lin, and the other animals the same. Maybe more cows though."

"You couldn't very well have Primrose and Kitty and Lin," I said. "But you could have Primrose's granddaughter or great-granddaughter. After all, we had her grandmother once. Would that be as good?"

"Sure, it'd be O.K. But it couldn't happen, because you'd have to be here too. And if you were here, I wouldn't be doing it all."

We carried the discussion a long way from there, never losing sight of his dream. On the face of it this was the opposite of what I have said I want for my children. But in fact it was Alan, a seven-year-old boy, recognizing the future and translating it for himself into terms of the only pattern he knows thoroughly. He was saying that he wanted to repeat the pattern, but he meant that he had begun to look far outwards, to consider where he would go and what he would do.

"There are lots of places besides this," I said. "And lots of jobs besides writing books. You might try all kinds of things before you really find what you want."

"I know," he said. "I'd like to be a cowboy sometimes, down in Texas maybe. A real cowboy that spends more time on his horse than anywhere else."

Each spring the children go out to sleep in tents pitched in the orchard or some other place they have chosen. It is always a struggle to keep them from moving out much sooner than they should and this year, after being asked several times, I set a deadline. "I'll pitch the tents on May 24," I said. "Not before."

By mid-April the weather was warm. By May 1, winter was long forgotten. I did not pitch the tents, but they put up the camp cots and slept on them under the trees. It was a neat circumvention of parental authority, completely logical and fully justified by the weather. Around May 26 it rained a little, so for a night or two they moved into the tents I had pitched on May 24.

Living in the country, one is supposed to worry about schools. When Valerie first went to school, Elkhorn had about a hundred school children, four rooms, and four teachers. They were good teachers, so the school was good and she was happy there and learned well. The village has grown and the school has grown; there is bus transportation now and overcrowding so that the children attend in shifts; teachers change constantly, there are time-wasting educational fads and props, and a relentless fostering of mediocrity. But Valerie and Mary and Alan all go there, they like it, and I think the essentials of education are still there.

The choice one is supposed to make is between private schools and public schools. Discipline and moral training are better in private schools, or should be. Private schools teach more flexibly within sterner limits of real learning, but in a

nation committed to state education they are lost and struggling orphans of a dead age. A child raised in public school
has a thousand associations with its time and its fellows that
the private-school child cannot have. It learns about a true
cross section of the country in which it lives and will work,
and it knows other children in relation to their homes and
families as well as in relation to the school. These are important things. In spite of the shallow curriculum, geared to slow
minds and narrow ambition, the educational theorists have
not yet been able to dispense with the fundamentals of learning—children are still taught to read and write, add and sub-
tract, they still read a sort of history and study the elements
of science. And, if their minds are alert to grasp this and put it
to use, no more is necessary.

The unanswerable point seems to me that the public schools
of the North American continent have produced great numbers of fine men and women, including some who were truly
great and creative human beings. The schools themselves do
not make these people, but indirectly the system does. The
discipline and morality of a normally decent home are live-
lier and more real things than those of the finest private
schools. If parents themselves have anything of wisdom and
learning and appreciation, they can pass it to their children
more soundly and fully than the best of teachers. Life at home
is more natural, more realistic, and far richer than the clois-
tered and specialized atmosphere of a private school; children
are happier in it and grow better in it.

I have said that our children like school. They complain
about it, grow bored with it, say they don't want to go, and
repeat all the complaints that children have made about
schools since the first schoolmaster wielded the first birch rod.
But the fact remains that they are happy there. Elkhorn is a
fairly rugged place and some of us are fairly rugged people.

Yet there is in its school very little of the senseless traditional cruelty of both children and teachers that I remember in the private schools I went to. Perhaps this is loss, not gain; one survived the other, learned from it, overcame and forgot it. Yet I think better, more tolerant, more humane citizens will grow from Elkhorn's way.

Having children, it is hard to imagine life without them. There is refuge in the thought that it will be fifteen or sixteen years before Celia graduates from high school, but this house now is alive with the sound of them, full of their business, urgent with their needs. Without them life would be a twilight, half-lived, half-seen, without real problems, real defenses, or solid substance. Alan comes in as I write this to take the stapler from the desk for some obscure purpose of his own upstairs. Celia comes in after him and plants her little red wagon inside the door.

"Cee back soon," she says reassuringly. "Going fetch Dolly."

From upstairs an earthshaking roar of rage from Valerie. I jerk forward in my chair, ready for action, for rescue, first aid, whatever is needed. But the fierce words flow on and it becomes clear that Alan has torn something, something ephemerally precious. And now Valerie is here for Scotch tape to repair the damage. I suggest that the volume and violence of her remonstrance seem to me out of proportion to the incident.

"But, Daddy, he's always doing something like that. We can't have anything without his tearing it or breaking it."

"Know what I thought?" I ask. "I thought he'd taken that stapler and driven one in to the hilt—probably from behind."

She laughs for a moment, then collects her anger. "It's not funny, Daddy. You think everything's funny."

"I'm not kidding. I really thought he'd done that—driven it into your thumb at least. You shouldn't roar like that."

"I know. But . . . " An exasperated sigh, a flaunt of her blue-jeaned figure, and she is gone. There must be a hitch somewhere in Celie's affairs with her doll, because I have been alone now for a full five minutes. But Mary is here.

"Can Stewart stay to supper and you drive him home after, Daddy?"

"Sure," I say without looking up from the paper. "Why not?" Now I realize there's something phoney about that. She would normally have asked Ann, not me. She probably has asked Ann. . . .

These and many others are the things about children that the parents of all time have learned and relearned. They are the things that one used to hear one's elders speak of, but never expected to feel in one's own sophisticated, well-ordered life—annoyance, impatience, fear in many forms, many times repeated; the lift of the heart in pride and joy; the sense of inadequacy, of the frailty of one's own wisdom; despair at the slowness of reason's growth in them. But mostly it is joy, in round babies, in tall daughters and sons who grow, not in one's own image or into one's weak imaginings, but into themselves.

I sometimes think the only crime a parent can commit, short of not loving a child, is to try and force it into the realization of his own half-forgotten dreams. There is no reason why the child of any parent should excel, or even want to excel, no reason why it should ever be urged to strive and fight beyond its strength. A child, and the man or woman after the child, must strive within its strength, up to its own full realization. It must learn to feel and know the world about it, advance the world if it will, use the world so far as it must, understand the world as it can. Fulfillment may be in driving trucks as well as in signing treaties, in lying in the leaves as surely as in painting pictures. Let children only become themselves, using eyes and minds and senses, feeling and enjoying as men and women do, searching into the meaning beyond meaning if they aspire to, accepting the truth in light and color and movement before their eyes if that is more natural to them. Let them only be true to themselves, so that they have true selves to give. Let them be sure in this, feeling the strength of their sureness within themselves, not in relation to or in competition with other men and women, but in relation to an absolute standard their own hearts know.

This I wish for my children, not honors or rewards or riches, not the satisfactions of success or even of creation, but only this sureness, truly and solidly based, that makes them human beings, capable of sympathy, understanding, and tolerance. It is in them now and growing within them. They see things with their eyes, interpret them in their minds, understand them in their hearts, and often show them again to Ann and myself with the impress of fresh thought upon them. They reach beyond us more and more boldly to touch the world and give themselves to it. I wish the world joy of them. And I wish them a world no more difficult and dangerous than man has always found it.

THE GARDEN

A GARDEN, LIKE COWS, IS PART of the life a woodsman comes to when he settles down. I grew the first gardens we had with *Sudell's Gardening Encyclopaedia* in one hand and hoe or shovel in the other. They were not bad gardens and I was proud of their yield—so proud, and so promptly proud in fact, that when the time came to thin the first row of radishes I could not bear to throw the thinnings away. I transplanted them instead.

The very first garden was grown in the shade of half a dozen apple trees; space was limited and everything had a tendency to go to leaf instead of fruit. During August some horses and cattle got in and enjoyed the abundance of leaf, but the potatoes and carrots and beets were still worth digging. The next year I cut the sod away from a piece of ground in front of the house and did better. By the time we moved to the new house I was an experienced gardener and usually left Sudell on the study table instead of carrying him with me. I had begun to experiment with the less usual vegetables—globe artichokes, eggplants, various broccolis, melons, and squashes. I was successful with tomatoes. I knew the joys of transplanting things and seeing them start away without the slightest check, and the even greater joy of successfully rooting cuttings. I had established a nice collection of herbs. And I had proved my mastery of the sweet pea.

From the first I had felt that sweet peas belonged with a vegetable garden, because I remembered that John Kelly always grew them nobly there for grandfather, between banked rows of celery two feet high and magnificent onions as big as softballs. Someone told me they were difficult to grow really well, so I turned to Sudell and followed him faithfully from the start. I dug three-foot trenches, a foot wide, filled them with layer upon layer of manure and soil and wood ashes and lime and fertilizer, chipped my seeds, planted them two inches deep in March, trod the soil over them to the packed firmness that is supposed to prevent bud dropping. When the plants had sprung through I thinned them, then pinched back the leading leaves to encourage root growth. I brushed off laterals and pruned away tendrils and disbudded almost daily as the plants grew. And the result was a magnificence of bloom that far surpassed my reasonable hopes.

It is nearly ten years now since I grew sweet peas, but they are still the peak of my gardening achievement. One year I grew thirty-six named varieties and could pick full bunches of each every second day in the season, great bunches of rich, pure color in three or four or five bold blooms to each long stem. I remember the names of the best of them now and still feel the old excitement as I pass over them in the seed catalogues. Gigantic, finest and best of whites; Welcome and Headlight, brilliant scarlets; Ambition and Powerscourt, the faithful lavenders; Amethyst, clearest of blues, and Flag Lieutenant for darker blue; Red Boy, bold crimson; Mahogany, deep purple; Pinkie, old as Powerscourt, just as good; lovely Debutante, with its pale salmon-pink against deep cream. I could grow them all again, as well as I ever did, and shall some day to revive that multiplicity of remembered pleasures.

All this was in the years before Ann became a gardener. In those years she watched from the kitchen and only gradually learned that I would not pick peas until the pods were full, or cut lettuce and cabbage and cauliflower till the heads were big, or dig potatoes till the flowers had died. A cook and a gardener, I suppose, have never seen eye to eye on the readiness of vegetables for the table and never will, unless they are one and the same person. Sometime during the war years Ann took over the vegetable garden and she has run it ever since, to the great good of the household, while I attend the frivolous flowers and trees.

Ann's garden is a combination of planning and emotion, of science and poetry, of determination and delight. And it is success in abundance, at the right times, in the right quantities, for the right purposes. Her finest crops are beans, peas, tomatoes, and corn and these set the times of her summer. But with them and among them are all the other vegetables, grown and calculated not with a gardener's pride but with a housewife's careful sense of the year's needs—spinach, chard, asparagus, and rhubarb for the early spring, lettuce, spring onions, young carrots for the first summer salads, broccoli, cauliflower, globe onions, young beets for high summer, cabbages and Brussels sprouts and some of the others again in the fall, leeks, Jerusalem artichokes, squashes, and all the mature root crops for winter.

Such is the garden's yield in framework and bold outline. But it is trimmed and decorated again with a good cook's seasoning of herbs: sweet basil for tomatoes, tarragon and dill for pickles, parsley and rue and thyme and sage, borage and hyssop for summer drinks, caraway for cakes, horseradish for beef, mint for mutton, garlic and chives for salads, rosemary for the housewife's prestige, lavender for closets and drawers, horehound, tansy, and wormwood because I planted them once and they still grow. And because a house must have flowers inside as well as out and any good vegetable garden must have color, she grows asters and stocks and zinnias and salpiglossis.

This is no mere generous yield of deep black soil. Our soil is light and sandy, easy to work and well drained. But it needs added humus and lime and fertilizer, steady care and building to make it yield well. The present vegetable garden was about five years old when Ann took it over and had already been built well above its normal productivity. But Ann has improved it relentlessly, with manure and compost, by plowing in green cover crops and experimenting with fertilizers. She has become expert with sprays and dusting compounds and hormone sets. She knows her way among the hybrid corns and can estimate the worth of a new variety of tomato with unfeminine precision.

Fifteen years ago Ann was a city girl, only a little while out of university and developing nicely in her job in one of the best bookstores on the Pacific Coast. She was a convinced intellectual, better read than most professors of English, altogether confidently and securely of the great world. She was, her sister Mary said, far to persnickety about things like underwear and modern poets and fine music ever to make a good country girl; and I had in my own mind a feeling that although we were starting out to live in the country it would be only a matter of time before we turned to a city. But I have never once heard Ann regret the city or suggest going back to it for anything longer than a quick visit.

She says this is because she has the heart of a peasant. Perhaps she has. She has also the mind of a seventeenth-century poet, the manners of a charming American, the emotions of Tolstoi's Natasha, and the strength of Saint Theresa, and while none of these qualifications excludes a peasant heart they do, at times, obscure it. The peasant heart is European, and not less noble for that. The American echo of it, strong and clear as the original and far more complex, is the pioneer heart; and this, I think, more truly than the other, is Ann's heart.

She has the determination, shared by pioneer and peasant alike, to live by every last fraction of the earth's yield and the land's bounty, to let nothing waste, to store and provide and guard against the dangerous days that may always come. She has also the pioneer's broader vision of the future and the pioneer's resolve to preserve and build on the transportable best of the past. And she has in fullest measure all the feminine desires and instincts and intuitions that have made the pattern of the family the most secure unit of human existence. But over and above this traditional and emotional foundation she holds, in absolute control, a sophisticated and articulate conception of exactly what she is doing. She believes in what she calls the dynamism of domestic economy. In this belief, and in the power with which she makes it effective, is the full explanation of how she turned easily and naturally from city to country, without any of the cute resistance or coy affectation that the transposition usually calls for.

It is, of course, an intellectual conception, but at the same time poetic. It is a conception of flow, unceasing, inevitable, meaningful as anything in the world can be. Flow of years is in it, flow of seasons and of all the usual high-sounding things. Any woman can feel this and find intermittent comfort in it. But Ann feels it intensely in day-to-day things, finds it in all the unceasing repetitions of ordinary living. In simplest form it is flow of water, twelve or fifteen thousand gallons a month, through faucets to its various uses, through these to drains and earth again. It comes from the pastures, through the cow, into the milk pail, then in its separate ways to the children, into cream and butter and skim milk; and the skim milk goes out to the chickens and returns again in their eggs.

It is not an analogy to be strained, but to be broadly felt, lived with, controlled. Modern devices and modern techniques direct it, control it, use it. A planned modern kitchen is many channels of flow and Ann has planned and built her kitchen in this way. Dishes flow in daily succession, from shelves to table to sink and dishwasher and back to the shelves again. Vegetables flow from their storage to sink to stove to table; there is flow from the cold storage locker to the refrigerator, to the cutting block by the stove, and so to the stove iself and the table; cupboards and drawers and counters are planned to use flow—some open and are accessible from two directions, some from only one. Ann does not bake a cake; the things that go into a cake are in the cupboard directly above the counter where she mixes cakes; bowls and cake tins are there also, and the mixer is ready on the counter, the oven is two steps away, the cake drawer is under the counter. Somewhere along the line she steps in to control and direct the flow she has created, but even while she is doing so she will be controlling other streams—laundry through the washer perhaps, or children to school, or even one of my books through the typewriter.

Dust flows into the house on passing feet, out again through the vacuum cleaner; people flow through, are talked to, listened to, fed or given drinks, and go on their way. But the flow of the vegetable garden and the orchard is the steadiest and most powerful of them all. From the rotting leaves in the compost, through start of seedlings and the first young greens of the year, it is unceasing. It carries through the most barren months of the winter in the yield of the freezing locker and the preserve cupboard, of the apple shelves and root bins; and it goes on always in the health and strength and growth of the children.

The importance of the conception is not in its details. I have sketched them here only to make concreteness from an abstraction. The conception itself is faith and feeling, welcomed and used, giving meaning to the routines of daily living. It is much larger than any concreteness, for it embraces all increase, all growth that comes from this house, through the children, through ourselves, through every outside touch we have. It can be extended into the future, or traced back into the past through the inheritances and traditions that made it. Ann gathering corn for supper is not Ann, but Ruth; with her children she is Rhea and, being human rather than a myth, more than Rhea; setting the supper table she is Martha and Mary in one person, and is so because, though "careful and troubled about many things," she does not fail to understand them.

I had not thought to make Ann grow so richly from her garden—to have done so seems to make the garden more than it is. Ann grows from everything she touches and returns growth to it, and the garden is only a minor part of this work of making and maintaining a household that she has built so skillfully into a positive, dynamic thing, more challenging and satisfying than any job. Her belief in the richness and movement of life does not stop here; it stops nowhere because she is without restraint in giving. Here again she has a conception of movement and life and reciprocity—conceived, like the other, after the event, to explain a naturalness of behavior, not planned as an artificial goal to strive for. Like the other, it is a conception of flow, the merged alternations of giving and receiving that is femininity itself, unceasing, questioning nothing, only feeling and responding.

Let me be clear about Ann. She is neither goddess nor saint, only human and woman. For all her conceptions, her house does not always flow smoothly—there is too much flow, too much giving and receiving, too many children, too many visitors, too much husband. Things pile into chaos, flow breaks on chaos, sometimes in fiercest stream, then passes on to reunite and smooth out again. Ann is fiercely emotional, quick in judgment, strong and direct in action. She is, for instance, as militantly pro-Semitic as some people are militantly anti-Semitic. She is aggressively suspicious of all big business and all politics. She has anger that flashes like a drawn sword and terrifies us all before we can realize that it has been sheathed again, harmlessly, in the same flash. She is, as I am, a romantic with minor modern trimmings; but she is also that rare, un-fashionable thing, character in depth beyond the explanations of motive and influence and cause; and she has a moral purity that brings her instantly to right decisions while I can only hesitate.

Ann's matriarchy is never admitted—its essence is that it must be denied, because all her beliefs revolve upon the idea that my frailty is the guiding strength of the family; she teaches the children this and even half convinces me at times. But at times also we see through it. There was the time, shortly after I came back from the army, that Mary and I were sail-ing a model power boat in the sheltered water behind the wing dam. I would wind the clockwork motor, set the rudder, and send it on its curving course to miss as narrowly as pos-sible the swift current that ran past the end of the dam. In the end I set the rudder wrongly and the little boat rode out into the current waves. The motor spent itself and the boat tossed helplessly, at three or four miles an hour, towards the sea. We tried to catch it and missed, ran downstream, missed again, caught up with it a third time just above Uncle Reg's water wheel. This time it had to be saved and I waded waist deep into the current and saved it. As I came triumphantly back to shore I saw that Mary was crying.

"It's O.K.," I said. "I wasn't going to let it get away."

"But, Daddy," Mary said. "You're soaking wet. What *will* Mummy say?"

Ann's friends—and she has many—remembering her at the university or in the bookstore, remembering the quickness and rightness of a mind that can give a wise answer to almost any question, often ask why she doesn't write a book. "You're so smart," they say. "You've got so much to write about. . . ." I used, long ago, to ask the same question, but I no longer ask it. Ann is living a life that yields stronger creative satisfaction than any a mere artist can know, for it is the original pattern of all human creation. When the flow slackens, when the children are grown, when "the blood is thin in the throat and the time not come for death," perhaps Ann will write a book.

AUGUST

AUGUST IS A MONTH OF TOO
much change for me to be altogether happy in it. The days of
the first weeks are rich and golden, full of summer and life
and warmth, of children planning and playing, people coming
and going. But sometime late in the month one becomes suddenly aware that summer is old and almost over, that it is
nearly time for the children to go back to school, that asters
are blooming, too many things are ripening, the leaves on the
trees are set in a maturity already dry.

In a very real sense it is the year's passing, the culmination
of all that built or rested under the fall rain and the winter
snow, of spring's thrust and summer's bloom. Hot dry days
of summer renewed are ahead in September, lively days of
fall, and the pleasant, restful close in of winter. But there is
that week or so of summer's lapse, of unwilling concession
that another year is done. Mostly I think it is in the nearness
of the children's return to another year of school, in the end
of their summer's freedom. I like it less and less as the years
go on.

When I feel this way I nearly always find myself thinking of the Big Fir. The Big Fir is not a true fir, but a Douglas fir, a false hemlock, the tree that has made the economy of British Columbia and the Pacific Northwest. It is the last true giant of its kind in all this flat near the river mouth, six feet in diameter breast high from the ground, and around two hundred feet tall. Judging by the rings on stumps of other trees on the flat, it is probably a little less than five hundred years old. It stands in the open field we call the Big Fir Field, nothing else near it except three or four of its own seedlings, the largest of them now thirty or forty feet high, standing so close that they seem part of the tree itself.

The Big Fir is slowly dying. It is dying because it is old, because it has a disease woodsmen call conk, and probably another disease called stump rot. Yet it is alive only because it is conky. The first loggers with their oxen passed it by for that reason more than fifty years ago; their skid road went through not three hundred feet from it and I cannot imagine their leaving it for any other reason. Other loggers passed that same way later, taking the lesser trees that the first loggers had left, but they still did not touch the Big Fir and its even larger companion which stood over by the barn. In 1922, when a crown fire struck down the far side of the river and leapt across on a northwest wind to a ridge a quarter of a mile away, fire fighters felled the tree by the barn. But they left the Big Fir still standing.

The Big Fir itself has been touched by fire, so deeply touched that the eight-inch bark near the base is all burned away from the east side and the blackness of fire shows in crevices in the bark all round the tree. There are tentative axe marks here and there and many riflemen, at many times, have used the great trunk as a backstop for their target practice.

People often ask me why I don't cut down the Big Fir. "It's dying," they say. "Anyone can see that. And you'd get ten years' good wood out of it."

Sure, it's dying. No one knows that better than I do. I've been watching it for nearly twenty years now. The wind-flattened top was green when I first knew the tree, sparse but green. One year life no longer reached that far up the tree, the needles died and fell away, then the little twigs fell away and after them the branchlets, then a branch or two, then some of the bark from the main trunk. But that all took five years or more. The topmost twenty feet of the tree are dead now and the tips of the lower branches are dying one by one, but there are seventy or eighty feet of heavy green limbs still above the lowest hundred feet of clear trunk. My guess is the tree has another fifty years of dying ahead of it, or somewhat more than I have. So long as any part of it is green I want it to stand.

The Big Fir was a good-sized tree before *Hamlet* was written and has managed to hold not only identity but life far longer than *Hamlet's* author held either. More human identities have been lost in every year of the tree's life than the tree itself has shed seeds, yet as trees go this one is not such a great age. Looking up at it against the sunset sky of an evening well on in August, remembering that it is almost time for the children to start school again, that another summer is past of the few remaining summers they will come free from school and go back to school, I feel the tree's pitiless permanence. It has used another year towards its death and during the year has scattered two or three hundred pounds of broken wood from its dead top about the field; yet even to my eye, it is scarcely changed.

I do not hate the tree or resent it or even wish it different. In most moods I love it and admire it. If it were young and vigorous, I think I should not even resent its permanence. If it is only just mortal, it is also only just living. But its enormous substance, lasting so long, yielding so little, seems to emphasize how short a time there is to look at things, to feel and know and think things. That the tree has been dying ever since I have known it and will still be dying after I am dead focuses my gloomier moods upon it; if only it wouldn't spread its last moments over my lifetime and beyond both ends I could accept it with nothing but happiness.

As it is, the Big Fir has many splendid moments. In spite of the dead top and the great blisters of the conk high on the trunk, it remains magnificent. For over ten years, before I moved to this new room, my study window looked directly out at it. I used to watch its great green limbs moving slowly and easily in the southeast gales, against the clouds of the driven sky. The ducks pelt past it on such days and swing back into the wind. I have watched a hundred, perhaps a thousand, eagles perch in its topmost branches. I have seen it plastered with snow from ground to top, standing tall and straight in the sunlight, green and brown and white against a blue and white sky. On a day like this I have watched blocks of snow fall away from the high branches, explode into finest powder, and linger in a cloud of white all the way down the trunk.

I have watched flickers and pileated woodpeckers and downy woodpeckers search the crevices of the tree's bark for grubs. I have seen ravens in the tree and crows and many hawks. Early one morning, as I went over to the barn to milk, a great blue heron was perched on the dead top. I thought he would be the one I watched almost daily at his patient fishing in the eddy on the far side of the river. But then four others flew on slow wings from beyond the alders, circled the tree, and pitched there as the first one called to them. Three of the birds seemed clumsy and uncertain, and I judged them to be young ones. It is the only time I have seen five herons in any one tree, away from a herony.

Once the Big Fir was shaded by other trees as large and larger, packed all about it in the heavy forest. The Indians had a smoke house within a hundred feet of it then and beached their canoes within reach of its shadow. I have found myself fishing and swimming and planting seeds in the same shadow, and I have sheltered new-born lambs and nursed them to life in its lee. The first trail up the river passed near it and the first skid road and the first wagon road. It is only a mass of wood, pitch-seamed, diseased, and rotten, with no more than a spark of giant life remaining in a narrow strip of sapwood. There are probably a million other great trees like it on Vancouver Island, overmature, moribund, without significance except perhaps in the seed they throw. Only a sentimentalist could give importance to such a thing. Yet I shall look up at the Big Fir a thousand times or more before I die, and never without emotion.

VISITORS

IT IS USELESS TO PRETEND THAT anything is normal in Elkhorn during August. That is the month when the tourists come to catch the big salmon. They come in other months, to hunt grouse and deer, to fish for steelhead and cutthroat trout and the lesser salmons. But in August they come for the big salmon and they come from the ends of the earth, from Hawaii and Panama, from New Zealand and South Africa, from India, Ceylon, Siam, from

London, Paris, Cairo, and Rome. But mostly from California. It is the month when Hollywood knows Elkhorn and the Guaranty Trust knows it and the U. S. Navy knows it and the British Army knows it. On the license plates of the cars parked along the main street you can read the names of half the states of the Union. For this month of every year the little town is colorful, busy, prosperous and exciting. It gets its name in the papers and it stacks up a good bit of the money that will keep it going through the winter.

On the whole the townspeople, especially the newcomers, do not like to admit any such debt to the tourists. They prefer to talk grandly of industry (there is none, except the logging camps that have largely supported the place and built its slow increase over half a century) and of some vague future when the tourists will no longer be important. But we who have lived here through a depression have no doubt about the importance of the tourists, and the resort owners know it and the guides know it. The wiser businessmen see it clearly in their records over the year and know how much tourist money comes back to them from guides and others in the months when there are no tourists.

Years ago this big tourist month was the time when we expected to see our own friends. They came to stay with us or to stay in the camps and hotels nearby and it was a gay and pleasant month that made each year a fuller thing. Now, if we feel that we are a stronger influence than the salmon, we try to persuade our friends to come in some other month, any other month than August. For we do not own ourselves in August.

I have, over the years, written several books about fish and fishing. These have got around among fishermen, so rather a lot of fishermen, when they come to Elkhorn, decide to come up to the house and talk about fishing. Some just want to talk, some want to ask where and how and when to go fishing, some want me to tell them what kind of a peculiar fish it was they caught last night, some want me to autograph books, some just want to say hello. The result varies all the way from some of the pleasantest interludes of my life to some of the most depressing—and Ann usually has to share both or even, if I am away, pinch-hit for me on where to and how to and on fish identifications. One result is unfailing: I never get any work done in August.

The logical thing would be to go away, but two things prevent that. Some of the August people are old friends and we want to see them; and then it is always difficult to believe that it will happen again. They'll forget the books and quit coming, I think; but they don't. Besides, it looks like a soluble problem. Ann will answer the phone and tell them in hushed tones that the master is at work and cannot be disturbed. If the resorts want to send people up they must come only between five and six. And so on. But it doesn't work. People don't stand for that stuff about the master at work in this day and age, and anyway half the time they don't bother to phone. They ask at the corner gas station and come on up or see the name on the mail box and come on in. That name hasn't been repainted since the rural route first reached us, but there must be something they can see.

It happens to other writers, I know, and it happens to us in other months than August. But in August it is so concentrated that it is the most important factor in our lives. I had thought to write about the August moon in this chapter, or about a battle of spiders I once watched on my windowpane; but when I began to write I knew it had to be about the tourists. Time after time Ann and I wake up to an August day, look out at the sunlight and say to each other, "Nothing today. No one coming. We can get some work done." At the end of the day we sometimes remember what we said in the morning and count up the fifteen or twenty people who have passed through the house.

In sum, it is gain, not loss. Nine times out of ten they are charming, friendly, interesting, generous, and kind; and they are very good for us. But by the end of the summer we are both a little harassed, and thoroughly appalled by all the work we haven't done. I wish now I had kept count of the number of times I have walked to the foot of the lawn with a visitor and tried to think up some inoffensive answer to the inevitable question: "I suppose you catch fish right from here?" It must be in the thousands. I don't and it's not a very likely looking piece of water, but the inevitability of the question used to drive me almost crazy until I told Ann about it. For some reason that made it all right.

It seems unfair to write about the irritations of the visitors, yet these are the things most easily remembered—the ones who do not irritate, and even some who do, become friends and are remembered as friends, not visitors. Probably the most irritating ones of all—remember that every one of these affairs is a formidable interruption—are those who say they are "just killing time"; waiting for a plane or a boat or the fish to come in or the rain to stop. After those are the ones who think you will be entertained by their prejudices; an hour or so of "why I hate Roosevelt" or "what the niggers are doing down south" or "how the Jews are taking over the country." I admire Roosevelt, I find Negroes impressive and inspiring people, and nearly all the Jewish people I know are fascinating companions and outstanding in their work. I have to say so, with reasonable tact I hope; but I'd rather get on with the job.

Then there are the Important Anglers. Usually they have invented famous wrigglers or broken innumerable records or won fantastic numbers of little buttons and badges or thrown flies out of sight in competitions. And their tales of slaughter, occasionally with supporting photographs, are endless and appalling. For the most part they are big men, very heavy, very sedentary, very much flushed with the celebrations of so many successes. I try sometimes to visualize them wading a rough stream bottom, but it doesn't add up. I try to think of them getting some fun out of fishing, but that doesn't add up either; their fun is in getting something bigger and fancier than their fellow men. On the whole they are interesting but monotonous.

We have communist visitors occasionally, full of causes and intellect, but earnestly wanting a little fishing on the side. And we have visitors who ask, "When do you get any work done?" And there is the visitor who comes along and asks, "Do you sell fishing licenses?" Occasionally this is no more than a clumsy opening; more often it is someone with a queer idea of a magistrate's duties. The answer is, "No, goddam it, I don't." For some reason it is one of the more annoying things that happens, as annoying for instance, as the half-witted, half-shot Canadian voice over the telephone on a Saturday afternoon asking, "Do you marry people?" No, and I don't make out wills or collect debts or write threatening letters. Some people think a magistrate should have as many lines as a cut-rate drugstore.

Sometimes August brings interesting combinations into the house. The capitalist sits down to dinner with the socialist and both stay happy. The trout fisher gets together with the big-game fisherman and both try to understand each other. An English peer meets a Middle Western manufacturer and each is surprised to find the other human. Once a stage designer and a young painter came in from a Hollywood yacht. They were fun and conditions were right for a party, so we had a party. At the height of it two old commercial fishing partners of mine turned up. They were heading south at the end of a long trolling season in a forty-foot boat; unshaven, greasy, but in high good humor. For just a moment I hesitated. The Hollywood boys had never for a moment left any doubt as to how matters stood between them, and I had a pretty good idea of how Mac and Joe viewed that sort of thing. But one doesn't turn old partners away for any reason that I know of, and Mac and Joe were in good shape for a party, so good in fact that I thought they might not notice everything, or noticing, might be tolerant. It went beautifully; everyone liked everyone, laughed with everyone and at everyone. The mood was so good that it held while the handsome young painter peeled back his shirt and showed off his monogrammed undershirt, but I made a quick move to mix another round of drinks. As I broke the ice out of a fresh tray I noticed the painter settle himself comfortably beside Mac and Joe. The room was almost silent for a moment and his soft voice was loud and clear as he dug Mac in the ribs. "Say," he asked. "You two boys going together?"

I held my breath, wondering how quickly I could cross the room and break it up—if there should be anything left to break up. But Mac rolled back in his seat with a great bellow of laughter. "Sure," he said. "Bin going for years."

Then there was the young man who arrived soon after breakfast one morning. He persuaded Ann that he had something of great importance to tell me, that it wouldn't take long. He was very solemn and serious and hesitant.

"I've read your books," he said. "And I've been thinking about them. I've got a subject for you."

"Better not tell me," I said. "I'll never handle all I've got now."

"This is different. I don't want any pay for it. I just want to tell you about it. You've got so much ability, you could do a lot of good in the world."

The approach was a little different, but the angle comes up once a month. "No," I said. "It keeps me busy just to write my own ideas."

He went on as though he hadn't heard me. His eyes were on something far outside the room. "You must bring religion into it. You don't know how much good it would do. Religion in a story, just like an ordinary book that people read."

"*The Robe*," I said respectfully. "By Lloyd C. Douglas."

His eyes focused on me almost sharply. "Yes," he said. "That's it. How did you know?"

I've never had a more sincere compliment—or a less accurate one.

I can come close to hating myself for writing like this, yet it is part of the way we live, an important part, and it won't be left out. Let me remember all the people who pass through and are too shy or too thoughtful or too gentle to come in. Sometimes they write to me afterwards, sometimes they send messages by others less shy; one man, whose name I still have not learned, left a bottle of Old Bushmills for me at the sporting-goods store. I salute them because their forbearance is the clearest possible evidence of their quality and courtesy.

And I regret them, too; their worth is so real to me because nearly all of those who do come in are so charming. I have met many good fishermen that way, men who have taught me a lot and some with whom I now go fishing every year. We have made many firm friends that way, and had many short encounters that made everything seem a little bigger and brighter and better than it had seemed before. And we have seen into many ways of life about which we might otherwise have known nothing.

Ann says that in some of the encounters I have behaved

very badly and only the tolerance of the people we met allowed things to turn out well. The Bostonians were up the river fishing and when I first saw them I was delighted. They were young people, man and wife obviously, beautifully equipped with rods and reels and nets and waders of the best and latest design. It was a good day and I had done well; it seemed a perfect chance for once to put the right people on to a good thing. But they stopped and began to fish below me. I saw they had chosen a gloomily unproductive spot and that they couldn't fish. When I came down to them they asked to see what I had caught, admired the fish, then sighed and said, "It's the same everywhere we go. We've been to all the best streams in the west and haven't caught a thing. What do you suppose is wrong?"

"Hell," I said. "That's easy. You can't fish. Come along to the house tomorrow and I'll try to show you something about casting, anyway. Fifteen or twenty minutes will make all the difference in the world."

Ann says that's no way to talk to people. But they came and everything worked out beautifully and we enjoyed them no end. Much the same thing happened once on a very remote lake—remote, that is, unless you fly. These people had flown in and we found them comfortably camped on a lovely creek where the fishing is always good. They were charming people, on their honeymoon too, and they offered us the choice of a Manhattan or a Martini as soon as we arrived—something that has never happened to me in the woods before. But they were crowding right on top of the fish, thoroughly scaring them, their tackle was no good, and they couldn't fish. I told them all that. "It's a darn shame," I said. "To come all this way and spend all this money, then not get your fishing because you haven't taken the trouble to learn something about it first. I'll bet you didn't start out playing golf that way."

I fished then for a little while and when we left to go on to the next creek I told Ann, "That was a very pleasant meeting."

She laughed. "You weren't very nice. If I ever throw my weight around like that people get furious at me."

"I don't think they minded."

"Of course they didn't. Couldn't wait till you got out of hearing to tell me how charming they thought you were. But I still don't see why it works for you and not for me."

"I didn't say anything that didn't make sense."

"What would you think if some stranger came along and told you whatever you were doing was all wrong?"

I know the answer to that. It happens quite often—book reviewers, for instance, and I don't like it a darn bit. But then most book reviewers can't fish.

Fishing seems to attract military minds. There was the Marine colonel who came one day when I was out. Ann has a special for her fellow Americans, to make them feel they are really abroad, and since it was about the right time she pulled it out of the hat. "Would you like some tea, sir?" she asked in her best English manner.

The colonel started violently. "Tea?" he roared. "Hell, no." And by that she was reminded there was whisky in the cupboard.

There have been courtly admirals, R.N. and U.S.N., splendid generals, gentle lieutenants. But the greatest of them all was the small quiet man who had been at Yalta and Teheran and Quebec and Dunkirk, who had watched Churchill's first meeting with Stalin and sat at Churchill's right hand through the most brilliant days of the war. He wanted a big salmon and it was an awkward time of year to find one and we didn't find one. In the short two days we fished he told generously and simply of the war years, so that the great names became living men—angry men, stubborn men, brilliant men, difficult men, warm-hearted men, each one obsessed with his own obsessions, each with his own abilities and his own limitations. Telling all this, he was completely fascinating and completely natural. But he told it only at intervals. His real concern was for a flight of American mergansers passing overhead, a raft of western grebes out on the bay, the flash of a belted kingfisher across the river, the croak of a raven high on the hillside, or the soaring flight of a bald eagle against the mountains. I am sure that few birds passed his sight and recognition in the tense years when he traveled the defenses and conference places of the free world.

Doctors also seem to be enthusiastic fishermen and I can't remember one we haven't thoroughly enjoyed. They are also exacting readers and know exactly what they want, so much so that I'm going to dedicate the next fishing book I write to the medical profession. If I can provide them a little entertainment it will be a small return for all Ann's determined probing of the latest theories of child feeding and child care.

Writers come occasionally, not as often as I would like, but when they do come we go most thoroughly into all the intricacies of our art—advances, percentages, reprint rights, film rights, serial rights, the law of libel, and the complications of foreign income tax. We discuss whether to autograph or not, whether to lecture or stay home, who makes money and why. One short evening with my fellow writers always restores my faith in the future of North American literature as a good sound business risk. But when I wake up next morning I never can remember why.

Ann says that after all this, no one will ever drop in on us again. I don't think I'd like that, so I can only hope she's as wrong as she is about the things I say to people when I meet them out fishing.

SEPTEMBER

Somewhere around the middle of August Ann begins putting meals on the table of which she can and does say with some pride, "Everything came off the place." By September it is no longer a matter for comment. The month brings a full flood of plenty from orchard and vegetable garden and pastures, from the river and from the woods.

Usually there is a three-day southeaster and rain during the first week of September, to mark the break between the full, steady strength of summer and the new vigor of fall. The storm passes and the sun seems as hot as ever, but the rain has sprung the dew and mists raise from the pastures and the river at night. Very often mid-September is forest-fire weather and sometimes there is a hard dry wind that shrivels the leaves, dries them up and rattles their bones, then tears them away like the dead bodies of Indians from burial trees. That is a time to worry and watch the sky for the great bursting cumulus of smoke that signals a fire out of control.

But in most years the night dews and mists are enough

to soften the threat of the gleaming days, and the warmth and brilliance is as welcome as any weather in the year, ripening the harvest, yielding it dry and unspoiled to cellar and barn and roothouse. And the rivers hold low and the hills are hot under the sun and the grouse spread out along them.

In September the pileated woodpeckers seem to show again about the place and the bluebirds pass through and the first great flocks of ducks sweep southward down the channel and over the islands. The humpbacks and spring salmon have come into the river and the broad-backed cutthroat trout, golden bellied, orange finned, are with them. This year a quick run of brilliant silvery rainbows came up too and the river held low all through the month and it was a simple matter to find three or four good fish with a floating fly almost any evening.

And September is the start of the hunting season. For nearly twenty-five years now I have worked the Vancouver Island opening of blue grouse and blacktail deer. Long ago it seemed automatic, inevitable, part of living. A buck dropped and brought in on the first of the season, and venison always in the larder from then until the end of winter. It was a food supply at least as essential, easier, and more natural than any yield of farm or vegetable garden. Sometimes we worked the opening of the season professionally, as guides or as hunters for a party of surveyors. Sometimes it was simply for ourselves and the relatives or friends we lived with. It was sport and part of manhood, but as little out of the ordinary as sawing and splitting the winter's wood supply. There were no roads in that northern country.

Later, when I came south on the Island to the roads, I was still a hunter and still with hunters—older men than myself for the most part, who had been hunting meat for their families for forty or fifty years. It was still as natural to go out, simply a part of the routine of life. But I cannot remember

that I ever found any deep satisfaction or real pleasure in the
hunting of Vancouver Island deer. It was good to be out in
the woods, as it always is, but I was in the woods all the time
in those days anyway. It was good to have an intensity of purpose in working out the habits of deer, their movement from
the high places, their choice of resting places and feeding
places, the effect of predators and breeding season, their re-
sponses to sound and smell and sight. But the find and the
shot seemed always anticlimactic, prelude to the dull and
rather unpleasant work of butchering and packing.

I had taken the training well, though, and when I first married Ann I told her there was no butcher store in Elkhorn,
and believed it too. One bought bacon at the general store and
for the rest one caught fish, hunted deer and grouse and ducks,
and occasionally bought a quarter of a beef or lamb or veal
that a neighboring farmer had slaughtered. After about a year
of this Ann discovered a perfectly good butcher in the village. I was deeply shocked at first; I felt we were well on the
way to decadence and debt. But the old Scottish butcher was
a very good man indeed and Ann learned quickly from him;
the monthly bills were not too impossible to meet and, once
I had learned to take Uncle Reg's bitter comments, it was a
relief to have the rifle in its rest. I have not killed a deer for
fifteen years.

Wing shooting was another matter and I stayed with it,
liking the close, intricate work of the dogs, the companionship
of a good friend, the long days of walking the rocky hills.
The roads were few and scattered in those days and hunters
were few—it was easy to pick country where one could walk
steadily through a whole day and see no one else. It was good
and necessary to be out in the fall days, working over logged
and discarded country, watching the start of new growth,

crossing ridges, finding creeks and swamps unseen and untrodden by humans between hunting seasons.

But the deer and blue grouse of Elkhorn became famous almost suddenly. There was the great fire of ten or eleven years ago, followed by fresh growth of salal and blackberry vines and huckleberry, feed and brouse of all kinds over a hundred square miles; then a multiplication of grouse and deer in proportion to the feed and a multiplication of roads through truck logging and reforestation. Three or four thousand hunters come now in their cars on opening day to hunt country that no more than thirty or forty of us worked a few years ago. It's more like the opening of a race track or a football stadium than the start of a hunting season. Hotels are full, newspapermen arrive, every side road has tents pitched along it, society (judging by the newspapers of the previous week end) is out in force. So are the tin-canners. Men who wave bottles out of car windows as they drive by, who leave ragged camp sites and broken glass to cut the feet of better dogs than they will ever own, who break down gates that are supposed to close off private roads, men who steal logging equipment and boats and skiffs, who break into cabins and hunt from cars driven slowly along back roads.

Somewhere in all this wearing of scarlet clothing, this boasting of bag limits, shipping of game through cold-storage lockers, searching of cars by game wardens at road blocks, the opening of the season has come to mean only a good day to stay home. There's time when the hotels are empty and the camps have been struck and the cars have gone south, to hunt the empty hills and find the grouse scattered over them. The dogs work better then, ranging widely to find single birds and small coveys. One walks farther for less shooting, but there's gain in that too. Nowadays I watch closely the growth of seedlings, the success of new plantings, the spread of alders from the low places. It will not be so very long before trees begin to take over again through most of the big burn. It will be harder then to find deer and many of the city hunters will stay home or go elsewhere. The grouse will not multiply quite so freely; a man will have to know the country and hunt well to find them. Most of the old logging grades will be grown up or washed out by then and the car hunters will have to do their hunting on foot. In ten or fifteen years the opening of the season may seem as quiet and normal as it used to.

STAYING FREE

Twenty years ago the average English-speaking family had little reason to fear any gross interference with its freedom. There might be pressures of one kind or another, through jobs or blacklisting or discrimination; there might be political interferences or mild unfairness of many types. But all these things were slowly decreasing and the mass of law increasingly favored true personal liberty—even the Sacco-Vanzetti case led to sharp improvement in state law. One felt free and safe in freedom. The father of the family, stirred by some single issue, might find liberty a good subject for a few weighty pronouncements, but in all probability he would be worrying for others, not himself. It seemed that in the western democracies liberty was soundly based, the state powerless against it.

Since 1933 all that has changed. The Germans showed plainly that the twentieth century has the deadliest means in all history of destroying personal liberty. The clearer picture of Russia that has developed since the war confirms the dead-

liness of everything that Hitler did and suggests that an efficient modern tyranny may be able to destroy even "the
people's divine right of revolution," to borrow the phrase of
a lawyer friend. The world has seen a new series of persecu-
tions, a new succession of martyrs in numbers never before
dreamed of. The details of mass killing, mass deportations,
mass compulsion of all kinds are given explicitly in the family
newspaper and the family magazines. A whole new morality,
diametrically opposed to many of the major concepts of
western civilization, is common intellectual currency, given
serious consideration and the full weight of the harsh force
that has established it. There is no need of a Huxley or an
Orwell to diagram it all. And there is no way of disregarding
it. If one wants to go on living in ordinary freedom and in
the hope of an expanding freedom for one's children, one
has to worry.

Down on a family and individual level it seems at first a
pathetic effort, funny and hopeless. Surely here is an issue for
princes and leaders of men, for orators and great writers, for
arms and armies and lawgivers, for all the weight and ingenu-
ity of man's organization and administrative powers! Yet in
reality it is purely an issue for families and individuals. No
army will ever again win perfect freedom for the people that
support it; lawgivers spend more of their time restricting freedom than extending it; a great leader should have little effect
upon a people that has a true understanding of freedom.
Masses of individuals save and build freedom, by wanting it,
by understanding its nature, by being able to laugh at themselves and every frill and fancy of government they set up.

It is not so easy to be free. One must first be free to think
and then able to think freely. Freedom of thought grows
somewhere out of the long slow history of western civilization, and it is bound by certain moral precepts that have stood

the test of centuries and stand the test of day-to-day living: these are matters of honor and honesty, of belief in the worth of man as a man and so in the sanctity of human life, matters of faith, of human sympathy, of tolerance, of loyalty, all the things that go to make human behavior predictable to the point at which men can deal safely with one another. To be able to think freely one must understand these things, their origin and their worth; and beyond that one must have some understanding of the nature of truth, of the variability of dogma, of the steady growth and change of all phases of human thought.

It is hard to achieve all this late in life, so I believe that the first obligation of a family that believes in freedom is to ensure that its children are taught these things both in school and at home. And I believe that this obligation is more urgent now than at any time in history, because the technique of lies and the dissemination of lies has reached a peak of efficiency never before known.

It is easy to write of freedom in high-sounding terms and generalities, far more difficult to live it. As a family we believe that all prejudice is a highway to slavery. I know we believe this, each in his own fashion; I know we understand it, each to his or her own capacity, at forty or thirteen or eleven or seven. But it is enormously difficult to be completely tolerant and unprejudiced, and none of us is or is ever likely to be. One has to have some convictions to be a worthwhile human being at all, and the dividing line between the virtue of conviction and the vice of prejudice is often too fine to be measurable by the owner of either.

This on the broad plane, towards an ideal; in the narrower plane of daily living we are both more and less certain. We are not politicians, though we follow politics quite closely. I vote conscientiously, but rarely go to a political meeting of any kind because the local people believe, most honorably I think, that a magistrate should not reveal any political preference. Ann, preserving American citizenship, does not vote in Canada, though she holds stronger political convictions than I do. The children will vote when the time comes and I know they will vote independently, out of their own thought and effort.

We speak, all of us, publicly or privately, as the need arises, against prejudice, which is easy enough to do and not always ineffective. We have done our little part, with pleasure, to ensure that Indian children are taught in the same schools as our own. We go to some length to try and learn the problems of unpopular minority groups such as the Doukhobors so that we can speak and act intelligently if the matter comes directly to us. We have been and are rigidly and openly opposed to the treatment of Canadian Japanese on the West Coast. We are, in fact, prejudiced against prejudice. If people are in a minority and in trouble we assume they have a case and a cause.

There is no special virtue in all this. It is rooted in self-preservation, because everyone is a minority and a member of several minorities—his family, his church, his trade or profession, the organizations he belongs to, his city or province and, ultimately, his nation. Under modern conditions it requires only a minimum of imagination to realize that he can be attacked at any or all these points. And once that is grasped the importance of minorities becomes an emotional and intellectual conviction.

I think often of our Pacific Coast Japanese, because the end of their story is not yet written. They were peaceful, reasonable, competent people who worked mainly in the fishing industry and did a great deal to develop it. Shortly after Pearl Harbor they were all moved away from the coast, twenty-three thousand of them, men, women, and children. Undoubtedly this was a perfectly sound military precaution. The Japanese accepted it calmly and cooperatively, with a humorous resignation of which any people might have been proud. There were men among them who had won decorations for bravery with Canadian troops in the first war.

Whatever military necessity may have been behind the move was dead within a year. Within that time the whole number of them could have been screened and checked and all but a few could have been safely allowed to return to their jobs, their businesses, their boats, their homes on the Pacific Coast. But Pacific Coast people were afraid of their competition and did not want them back. So their property was sold and most of them were herded into camps. And they were not allowed to join the armed forces; only civilian and political pressure was responsible for this.

In 1945, shortly after V-E Day, we came back to form a Canadian force that was to have taken part in the invasion of the Japanese main islands. Almost immediately it became apparent that we were hopelessly short of interpreters. Intelligence officers went out among the Japanese and in a short while were able to find the hundred or so young men needed; nearly all of them had previously tried several times to enlist, but offered themselves willingly again.

It seemed reasonable to suppose that immediately after V-J Day any Japanese who wanted to would be able to return to his life on the Pacific Coast. But for nearly four years longer, using special war powers, the government kept them away. Not because there was danger from them; there clearly was not and had not been for six or seven years. But because of political pressure from ordinary voters, fishermen, small fruit growers, market gardeners, small businessmen, who did not want them back. The small local oganizations were passing resolutions against the return of the Japanese, but Elkhorn's did not. I once attended a meeting called especially to discuss the matter. The local M.P. was there. On the way down my friend Alec, whom I admire as much as any man I know, said, "Don't talk tonight, Rod. Those fishermen are liable to do anything—take you out and throw you off the wharf." For an hour I listened to bitter, intemperate chatter from men I know and like well. "There'll be bloodshed if they come back," one said. "We'll take out the thirty-thirties, that's all." "You can't work with them. They aren't like white men." "There'll be bloodshed if they come back," said another, grinning.

So I stood up and spoke, directly to the member. He knew what I meant. I know and knew what I was talking about, because I've worked with Japanese in a sawmill and have fished beside them. Scarcely anyone else seemed to understand, though no one suggested I should not say what I had to say. When I was through a young and pretty girl stood up and supported what I had said. She was an English war-bride, not two years in the country.

The Japanese haven't come back yet, though they are free to do so now. I think some of them will come, and I wonder how it will be.

Nothing done on this scale is big or of high importance, but it is not a family's business to be highly important, only to be direct and sure and informed in dealing with what is nearest. To speak or keep quiet on matters of prejudice and discrimination is not a question of courage or cowardice—now —but of judgment; and after judgment, emotion. Prejudice itself is founded in emotion, usually in fear, and the natural response to it is emotion, the simple emotional recognition that all men have the same love of their lives and possessions and places.

September

I am never sure how secure Canadians are in freedom. There is a feeling of danger in being a young country, with only a short history to build tradition, only a few people from among whom to choose wise legislators. It has been suggested that we need a written Bill of Rights in addition to the inherited protection of British common law, and I think that possibly we do. The British are sure and wise in self-government as is no people; they have shown many times that they understand freedom and will never let it go; their sense of history and of themselves makes the protection of political usage, statute law, and common law safer and stronger than any written law can be. But perhaps we need something to point to and shout for; something to build on as the Supreme Court builds on the United States Constitution. I should like them to talk it out in Parliament. It is the sort of issue any parliamentarian should be proud to work over, and here is one tax-paying family that would follow every gilded word of such a debate.

How far liberty can slip, almost unnoticed, I learned three or four years ago when I tried to buy a copy of Edmund Wilson's *Hecate County*. I did not know about the erotic page or two at that time; I knew of Wilson simply as one of the most learned and interesting literary critics I had ever read and I was intensely interested to see what sort of a book his knowledge of literature would produce. But the bookseller told me: no, the book was banned in Canada. I couldn't have it.

"Who in hell banned it?" I asked. "I haven't seen anything about it."

"Customs won't let it in. It's not printed up here. You can't have Joyce's *Ulysses* either; that's banned."

"I've had it for years. Nice cheap copy too—Modern Library."

"Sure," he said. "Sure. But you've no business having it.

Someone in the customs decided it was dirty or subversive or something. Maybe figured it was code."

That started me on one of the funniest correspondences I have ever enjoyed. I began with the Minister of Justice, was quickly shifted to his Deputy and from there to Customs and Excise. What I wanted to know was who they had on the staff who was qualified to pass on the literary quality of a book by Wilson or Joyce; I felt he must be quite an erudite individual and one well worth knowing in view of the general lack of literary criticism in Canada. What they wanted most to tell me was the number of the clause under which they had power to ban books. Item 1201, Schedule C, of the Customs and Tariff Act, they told me in letter after letter. Occasionally they even quoted the comprehensive words: "Books, printed paper, drawings, paintings, prints, photographs or representations of any kind of a treasonable or seditious, or of an immoral or indecent character."

But I was very persistent, and finally they told me that there was a man called "the Examiner of Publications" who made all the decisions. I gathered he was an elderly gentleman, because he had gone off on superannuation leave soon after turning thumbs down on Edmund Wilson. The Department was, it assured me, satisfied that he had the qualifications necessary to pass on books of a treasonable or seditious, or of an immoral or indecent character.

Unkindly, I said I doubted it. What, I asked, of *Ulysses?* Didn't it seem like a fearsome load of responsibility for one man to take on his shoulders?

The Department thanked me for my interest and said it thought it was doing fine.

"What," I asked again, "of *Ulysses?*"

"In regard to James Joyce's book *Ulysses,*" the Department wrote, "I understand it has been on the prohibited list for some time. We have not on file here a copy of it and, consequently, it is not possible to reexamine it. . . . I assure you," the Department added, "that the Department is doing its best to administer this tariff item fairly and equitably."

One has to admire such skill in creating a private vicious circle; ready at hand to ensure frustration when frustration seems desirable. But I thought of Joyce and others on the Department's list—Burton, Balzac, de Maupassant, Farrell, Trotsky, D. H. Lawrence, Pierre Louys, Radclyffe Hall—and I searched out Milton: "We should be wary therefore what persecution we raise against the living labours of public men, how we spill that seasoned life of men, preserved and stored up in books." And, still the words of the great Puritan: "Consider what nation it is whereof ye are, and whereof ye are the governors: a nation not slow and dull, but of a quick ingenious and piercing spirit, acute to invent, subtle and sinewy to discourse, not beneath the reach of any point the highest that human capacity can soar to." Or is that less true of twentieth-century Canada than of seventeenth-century England? Perhaps it is. A nation that cries daily to heaven for a literature, then denies its writers the study of Joyce because there isn't a copy on file, can scarcely have earned that voice, these words.

It is not hard to find things within the state to fear; there are many besides these, old things that have been fought and won before, new things that are harder to fight than the old. All legislators, all governments perpetually encroach upon liberty; it is hard to frame laws that will convict the guilty yet leave the innocent secure in the age-old protections. The smaller the legislature and the less skilled the legislator, the more dangerous will be the attempts to circumvent the protections; attempts made perhaps in clumsy innocence and well-meaning ignorance but always carrying danger with them.

The only protection, ultimately, is in a people that knows liberty, understands its nature and wants it. It is a matter of many little watchings, in many families. Liberty by grace of government and not by right is not liberty.

And when all is said that can be said and done that can be done for liberty within the nation, the monstrous twentieth-century threat of total war from without remains. Again it is a matter for the voices and thoughts of families and individuals, breaking through somehow, anyhow, to express that only wish of decent men everywhere: freedom to live fully the life that is before them, according to their individual consciences and without hurt to others. If the wisdom of small nations can be spoken with weight that matches the power of the great nations there will be some hope. If not, a family may be wise to teach its children some of the primitive arts of living and survival.

OCTOBER

It is easy to forget, between seasons, the brilliance of the maples across the river in the fall. They are big trees and they mount the high, steep bank in mass after mass of brilliant gold, taking it over so completely that one is scarcely conscious of the other trees. And they are reflected again in the surface of the river, gold against blue, broken by the current breaks and the splashings of salmon, full of the sense and meaning of fall. There are the broadleaf maples of the coast, despised of loggers, too western to have become the Canadian emblem, yet fully as lovely as anything I remember of eastern fall coloring.

October draws the eye towards the river, for many reasons and in many ways. Morning and evening mists come up from it, frail and lovely as they hang above the water or spread low across the fields. Salmon are moving through and spreading out to spawn. Ducks and gulls and eagles are returning. The coons come up from the river nightly into the orchard to compete with our reluctant picking for plums and prunes and apples. And the bears come, sometimes for fruit, always for salmon.

Bears, like most wild animals, cling very closely to their natural diet. Our bears feed busily on skunk cabbage and grubs and hornets' nests and berries and salmon in due season. Some of them kill fawns when they find them and some of the bolder and bigger ones' may try to rob a cougar of its kill. Only rarely does one bother sheep, yet we always worry a little because a bear that has once learned a taste for sheep can be a formidable problem. And they turn to orchards almost as rarely as they turn to sheep, which seems strange because they love wild crab apples and the salmon runs bring them right through the orchard along the river bank. There was one last year who liked apples. He went to Reg's orchard first and made himself happy with Gravensteins. Then the King tree was ripe, so he climbed to the top of it, lost his balance, and slid all the way down, breaking off most of the limbs. Reg was very angry and said I should shoot him or else he would. I waited one or two nights, very halfheartedly, and did not see him, so forgot about it. Then he came back and climbed our King tree and our winter banana trees, leaving only neat little claw marks on the bark to show he had been there and droppings full of apples to show he had got what he wanted. So I told Reg I found our bear a considerate and altogether acceptable visitor, very clever and delicate in his climbing. The bear that had wrecked his tree, I said, must be an entirely different creature, of grosser and clumsier breeding, and I would take no responsibility for him.

This year there has been no bear climbing apple trees; but one evening, when we were all standing on the lawn, a female came half-wading, half-swimming across the river with her cub close behind her all the way. We walked slowly down to the edge of the river, expecting her to turn and go back. But she came on very calmly and deliberately, slipping a little on the rocks at times, shouldering her way against the current in the deeper places, paying no attention at all to the cub who struggled and stumbled and hurried along behind, often swimming where she could wade. They were both very black in the evening light, seemingly unwetted by the water they passed through, completely preoccupied with the solemn concern of reaching whatever it was that they wanted on our side. They landed only forty or fifty feet from us and came up the bank under the Balm of Gilead tree, just on the other side of the hedge. I told the children we had better walk away a little, in case they should come suddenly through the hedge and our nearness make her afraid for her cub. We walked slowly up the lawn until we could see them both through the gap where the gate is. They were still concerned only with their own affairs, moving calmly towards the nearest pear tree. But there must have been a light drift of air from us to them, for the female turned suddenly in smooth and lovely movement and the cub followed her down to the river again. We watched as they crossed back to the other side and were sorry we had disturbed them. They have not been back again.

All through the year I watch the American mergansers across the river. I can see them at almost any time of almost any day, except perhaps in early summer when the males are away and the females are sitting tight on their nests. They are out with their broods in July and by August the young birds are well grown, still a little splattery and, by merganser standards, clumsy in the water, but already bold and competent as they dive and swim and drift among the rocks and shallow riffles. By October they are big as the female and almost indistinguishable from her. And in October the first males show up again.

The mergansers are purely fish ducks, with slender, toothed bills and a skill in diving and swimming that is beautiful to watch. They are also large and handsome birds, strong and swift on the wing once they are clear of the water, and it is only because their fish-eating habits flavor their flesh that they remain as numerous as they are. Fishermen are supposed to dislike them, but I do not; I think they do at least as much good in destroying predator fish as they do harm in destroying game and commercial fish; and even if I did not think so I should still want them to be numerous.

It is always satisfying to watch a creature that is perfectly adapted to its element and the mergansers have a beauty of color and line that would make them worth watching if they only sat still on the water. The female has a white breast, grey wings and back, a red-brown head and neck and crest; the male has a dark green head and neck, so dark as to be almost black except when the sun is on it, with the same color along his back and a breast of smooth salmon pink, unbelievably pale and delicate, yet so rich and deep in the texture of the feathers that the first close sight of it is something I still remember and always shall remember. And he is a proud bird, this drake, constantly preening and displaying himself, darting at the water with his scarlet beak, flirting the brilliant orange of his feet and legs against the pink of his sides.

Often, when the river is high, half a dozen mergansers collect in a little eddy on the far side of the river. I find myself expecting them to stay there, and look away after a while, only to look again in a few minutes and see them swimming easily upstream against the swiftest, most broken water. They seem like little canoes, handled by canoemen perfect in strength and skill. They are not against the water, but of it, accepting it, using it, delighting in it. Then, as though this surface swimming were altogether too simple, one dives, then another and another and another until they are all out of sight under the turbulent surface of the water. Long ago I used to watch for them to come up somewhere downstream of their dives, but I know now that I shall see them upstream, often ten or fifteen yards upstream, surfacing suddenly and matter-of-factly on the broken water, often diving again immediately to swim and fish their way out of sight.

Later they will come back, bobbing and swimming in the current waves, steering under perfect control to the eddy, where they will preen and fish and chase each other until some mood or hope of better fishing sends them out to work through the current again.

The yearly disappearance of the big drakes from the river right after the breeding season fascinates me. I usually notice them in the last two weeks of April, still in full plumage, grouped in sixes and sevens, without the females. Then they are gone. I have never seen them on salt water, as I often see the male harlequins during the summer months. I know the merganser drakes go into eclipse plumage shortly after breeding, and that in this plumage it is difficult to distinguish them from females, but I have never seen any ducks that I thought could have been them at this stage. Their reappearance on the river is sharp and clear, in late October, and by that time their green-black heads and backs are brilliant again and the heavy down of their breasts is gleaming white.

The river is very high today, so high that there is no eddy under the far bank and the largest rocks show only as a break of white on the sweeping surface. The speed of the current must be at least five or six miles an hour, perhaps more. A single female is riding it, right out in the center of the stream. She drifts with it, then suddenly dives in a looping forward movement that arcs her whole body clear of the water for a moment. For fifteen measured seconds she is out of sight in the murky water, then suddenly she is on the surface again, a yard or two upstream of where she went down. For five or ten seconds she drifts, then dives again. She deserves to catch fish.

TOOLS

I AM NOT EXACTLY WHAT IS called handy with tools, nor am I by any means skillful; but I am happy with them and can usually make them do what they are meant to do. Simple tools, I mean, that the hands work; nothing complicated or mechanical. The plain truth of it is, of course, that hand tools are very well designed; there isn't the slightest reason why any normally equipped human should not be able to make them perform fairly well.

Living in a forest country I am fully convinced that the greatest of all tools is the axe, double-bitted for preference, with a swamping blade weighing about four and a half pounds, and a thirty-inch handle. To make it fully versatile, one bit should be ground with a long tapering shoulder to a fine edge, the other filed or ground to an even edge backed by heavy shoulders that taper quickly. The finely ground blade can then be kept as a sacred trust, for clean, smooth chopping only; the sharply tapered edge will split safely, stand up against knots, break out twisty grain; it can even be chanced among roots and small brush—if a rock does happen in the way the damage is fairly easily repaired.

With an axe a man can build himself a house and all the furniture he needs. He can cut wood for his fires with it, clear his trails, split fence posts. He can use it to build a raft or hollow out a canoe, and it will serve as a weapon of offense or defense if he needs one. The axe clears land, lets in the sunlight, and if there were nothing else available, it could be degraded to the task of breaking and digging soil for the first garden. Surely no other single tool will go so far towards supplying man with the essentials of living.

I have never been a finished or a powerful axeman. I have built a small cabin with an axe, and many rough shelters, many rafts. I have felled trees, scored timbers for a bridge crew, cut line for survey crews, brushed out trails, built fences, cut poles, notched guy-line stumps, even topped a tree or two; but I have also seen men who could use an axe as a precision tool, hewing a smooth surface to a small fraction of an inch, notching logs so that they fitted into each other like cabinet-makers' work, and I have seen the same men chop and split and pile two cords of alder wood in a day or fell and peel cedar poles with a swiftness and ease that made me feel my own axe was a tool of some different, far inferior metal.

Yet even my limited competence finds an axe the most natural and dignified of tools, and the most satisfying to use. There is immense delight in a full, free swing, in the deep bite of the blade, in the spring of the handle under the hands and the gleam of clean narrow chips flung far out from the cut. The sound of an axe is good. The rhythm that grows into the work is good. The sharp smell of the fresh-cut wood, cedar or alder or fir, maple or hemlock, is immensely stimulating. Above all, I think, the simple effectiveness of the work is deeply satisfying. Nothing is set or precisely measured or narrowly limited, yet the notch grows swiftly through the mind's instant choice of where to drive the next stroke, the raft is built and shaped into easy balance under the eye's measurement, bark and sapwood slice away with no closer guidance than the hand's touch on the scoring stroke.

I became a carpenter, of a sort and to my own surprise, when my partner and I decided to build a cabin of lumber instead of logs. It was quite an ambitious affair of three rooms and it turned out astonishingly well in spite of the fact that we both turned to the axe whenever more orthodox tools seemed too slow or too cussed. I learned then that a saw cut has width and that one cuts to one side or the other of a penciled line and measures with this in mind. I learned that a nail can be driven to draw a board, that planes must be kept as sharp as axes, that square and level are important tools though they neither cut nor shave nor split.

When Ann and I bought a house we had very little furniture and no money at all left over to buy any. So my first job was to build half a dozen tables and a few shelves. I approached it with sincere misgivings; it was one thing, I thought, to saw boards and nail shingles and lay flooring for a frame house; tables had to be finished and fitted, with legs all exactly the same length, braces invisible, corners mitered. But the tables were fair enough, in fact some are still around the house, and I have pursued my modest carpentering with steadily increasing confidence right up to the present. After each book I give myself two or three weeks of it, to catch up on all the jobs that should have been done in the year that is past. After the long, slow, foggy struggle of the book it seems supremely easy, in spite of the occasional recalcitrance of wood or metal or space, and the results are unbelievably quick and impressive in proportion to the effort. For the moment I feel again that I am master of my fate, a fit person to put difficult things down on paper. The mood passes, of course, and I become my faltering self again. But occasionally Ann reminds me to look around and see my easy triumphs—tables, cupboards, lamps, beds, even this desk, mahogany surfaced and trimmed with gumwood, no less. The mind that drove the hands to such accomplishment cannot be wholly ineffective.

I have also become a plumber, of the simple or figure-it-out-and-fix-it variety, and I really enjoy wrenching pipe and working out combinations of elbows and T's and unions and valves to finish up approximately where I want them. Not that I tackle anything complicated; I have the greatest respect for the tools and skills and experience of the professional plumber. But the simple repair jobs to sinks and toilet tanks and washbasins, little matters like running a water line to the rose bed, are too tempting and satisfying to be missed. And the long years of trial and error with the intake from the river were something that only a devoted amateur could possibly have endured.

Most of the farm and garden tools are less dramatically interesting than the tools of the woodsman, the carpenter, and the plumber. But I like the effective design of manure shovels and hay forks and digging forks and I enjoy working with a well-sharpened shovel or hoe. I should like to have one of these small garden tractors, but am faintly suspicious of them; even a lawn mower, which seems a relatively simple affair of five revolving knives against a stationary knife, is a little too far over on the mechanical side. I push it around with fair satisfaction for a while, then suddenly find it is not doing too well. I do things to it then, with screw drivers and wrenches and oilcans and whetstones, and it seems to improve again. But I am never quite sure what I have done and know that I shall have to approach the same problem again soon, with the same doubts and hesitation.

Of all farm tools, the most admirable is the scythe. I am far from expert with it and have really no need to be expert because we keep sheep to do the grass-cutting. But I do not trust the sheep among my young trees and there are always corners and edges that they do not reach, so I use a scythe for a few days every summer. Mine is an old ridge-backed twenty-eight-inch blade that I inherited with the place and set on a new snathe. It sharpens easily and holds its edge well. I thought once that I might be able to work more smoothly and elegantly with a more ambitious tool, so I bought a really handsome blade, cracked it on a rock almost the first time I used it, and have still not learned to handle it as it should be handled. Perhaps, in a fine straight field of standing grain, I might be able to make it perform. But around trees and stumps, in the trampled mixture of grass and brush I have to cut, the little old ridge-backed blade is incomparable.

It took me a longish while to learn to make a scythe work at all. Then I learned to keep the point always well down, dragging it on the backward sweep; to work smoothly, cleanly, accurately, putting the right shoulder into the cut. And finally I learned not to try to cut too wide a swath. The thought reached me exactly through the proverb, as it ran over and over in my mind. My first reaction was to go right ahead and prove that I could cut as wide as any man. Then I realized that in my type of mowing there was neither need nor place for the wide swath; it calls for short sweeps, quite smooth, with the feet moving and the shoulder behind the snathe to drive cleanly through the unexpected resistance of broom or salmonberry or thimbleberry. And so I work and get my effect and please myself.

Very occasionally I come to a place where there is a hundred or two hundred feet of straightforward mowing ahead of me. Then, immediately, I am with Levin and the old *starik*, mowing my best, trying to keep to the smooth and steady pace between them, feeling the pleasure of the work as Levin felt it, recognizing each stage of effort as he did, remembering Tolstoy's superb statement of the meaning and satisfaction of hard manual labor. I come to the end of my row, shoulder my scythe, and walk back with the other mowers, thirty or forty of them in the huge field, to start a new swath. I work through the progression that Levin knew, from clumsiness and pain and challenge, to a competence that becomes concentration and absorption, sweat-soaked but full of rewarded effort, almost to the *starik's* easy mastery that makes the work part of being, pure pleasure of its own, with time for delight in every smallest thing that passes through the day. But the straight smooth going always ends too soon, turns me back to quick turns and short strokes around awkward places. Mastery is for the old *starik*, for the long fields and an older day.

I have not been able to avoid mechanical tools entirely. One has to have a water system, and of all mechanical things I suspect that pumps are the most mysterious and contrary. We started with something simple, a double-acting force pump mounted on a raft and driven by a water wheel. The raft sheltered behind a wing dam in the main river and to start the pump one simply winched the raft out until the current caught the wheel and started it turning. The pump forced water slowly but surely up into a big tank that fed the house by gravity. It was a good system, ideally simple and practically cost-free. The pump itself had only the most minor idiosyncrasies; within something under six months I had learned to prime it under all circumstances that could possibly arise. The length of flexible hose connecting the raft to the shore made occasional problems; it had a habit of flying off the end of the pipe that led to the tank as soon as one turned one's back, which left the poor little pump solemnly working its heart out to pour water back into the river; and it usually managed to collect enough water to block itself completely in freezing weather. But these were minor failures, easily corrected. Low water was another problem; sometimes the raft would go firmly aground, which meant half a day of prying out rocks with a crowbar. High freshet was a time of prayer.

First logs and chunks of wood came down to break the paddles out of the wheel and one knew it was time to remove the pump from the raft. Then the water would burst over the top of the wing dam and the raft would dance like a cork instead of the twelve good cedar logs it was. Then the outside cable would tear loose and the raft would be held by one corner, riding like a surfboard. This began the real time of prayer. But as the water rose and the great waves over the buried wing dam grew impressively higher and higher the raft would plunge for the bottom; through the next several days one watched anxiously for the occasional reappearance of the tip of the shattered wheel as evidence that the raft was still there, somewhere under the angry waters. Then, as the waters receded and the raft came to the surface again, there was the work of cutting away driftwood, repairing the wheel, and restoring the pump to its place. And so the house had running water again.

At least the problems of the water wheel were bold and clear. The next pump we had was a centrifugal monster driven by a horizontal, heavy-duty gas engine. In its better moments it hurled a deluge of water through two or three hundred feet of pipe to another big gravity tank. But its better moments were few and always fleeting. I fought it for seven years and somehow made it supply the house with water. Towards the end I had a measure of mastery, and pride will not let me remember all the details of my frustrations and defeats. I see them now in the light of bitterly won knowledge and cannot recapture the sensations of fury and utter helplessness that tore at me in the days of the pump's repeated treacheries. For a centrifugal pump will have no truck with anything less solid than water; given the least breath of air, it will lie down on the job; which means that the full length of the intake pipe must be full of water, every joint must be airtight, the foot valve must be leakproof, and you must prime the pump itself until it is solidly full and overflowing with water. Then you must swiftly and surely start the motor that drives it, making certain that the speed is right and that the belt is tight, without slip. Hundreds upon hundreds of times I have done this, precisely, exactly, efficiently and confidently; have then gone out and checked the foaming stream at a valve, closed the valve and gone happily about my business—only to realize ten minutes or an hour or two hours later, by the sound of the motor or the halt of the gauge on the tank, that the pump had found me deficient.

Time and again I made aggressive and competent moves that I thought would cure the trouble forever. It was a triumph when I shortened the intake pipe, reduced the number of threads and couplings that could suck air; another when I found that the magneto was weak and had it overhauled; still another when I realized that the vibration of the river current was loosening a gasket on the pump and put in a flexible coupling to reduce it. Towards the end I think I was nearly on top—only one thing had me still in doubt and that was the continual rise and fall of the river that meant almost constant changes in the intake pipe. I had some ideas, even for this, but when the time came to go to the army I knew it was too late; I could not leave Ann to face such a monstrous and perverted thing, so I put in an electric pump.

When I installed the electric pump I decided to cure the intake problem for once and for all by digging a well close by the bank of the river. But the water was hard and full of iron and Ann wanted no part of it. So after the war I went back to the unequal struggle with the river. Our river rises and falls a total of about twelve feet. It is always fast; in freshet time it carries silt and stirs rocks and sand along its bottom. A floating intake will carry away, no matter how you anchor it.

An intake close to the bank will silt up if you dig a hole, or go dry if you don't. One carried well out into the stream will pick up coarse sand and ruin your pump when the river begins to run hard. And however you cover your pipe, high water will uncover it and the frost will trap you when the river drops suddenly in a cold spell.

I did not win, but I achieved a compromise triumph by a two-way intake, a complicated matter of valves that switched to the well in high water, the river in ordinary water. Two or three months ago the village ran a pipe line past the gate and I let them hook me into it with a great sigh of relief. Then I waded out into the river to dismantle my complicated intake.

It was beautiful summer weather and as I worked with the pipe wrenches I knew that I was as happy doing that as I am out fishing. I like it in the river, always have liked it, even in freezing winter weather. The birds are there, the May flies and sedges are there; it's the same clear, strong-flowing current, the same rocks, the same sand, sometimes there are even fish around. Sorrowfully I counted all the bits and pieces as I took them apart: two brass foot valves, two $1\frac{1}{4}$-inch unions, one 1-inch union, one $1\frac{1}{4}$-inch T, sundry bushings, couplings, reducers, one $1\frac{1}{4}$-inch gate valve, one 1-inch ditto, several lengths of $1\frac{1}{4}$-inch and 1-inch pipe. Then a cheerful thought came to me. Ann already complains that the village water costs far more than any water should cost. But one could make the garden system operate. One of those smart little centrifugal pumps out of the catalogue, portable, with an air-cooled motor. Park it right down close to the river, with a short intake. Maybe an intake on a float would work just for a summertime job like that. I've always wanted to try it. . . .

ON MAKING A LIBRARY

ANN AND I HAVE ALWAYS BEEN buyers and hoarders of books. I cannot remember the time when I did not feel invitation from any secondhand bookstore, and I have scarcely ever been able to part with a book without regret. In time, this begins to mount up. After we were married we put our books together and found that we had several shelves of them, in spite of the wastage of travel and movement. When, after two years, we moved into our present house, the books were by far the heaviest and bulkiest item of our movement. We lined a small room with shelves from floor to ceiling, spread the books out and felt we had space for growth. Within three or four years we were finding ingenious ways of crowding in new shelves; within ten years the books were crowding us out of the room. Immediately after the war we built on a new and much larger room, lined it with shelves from floor to ceiling, and again felt we had room for growth. We still have, a little. But we are already discussing the place and design of future shelves. This amounts, I suppose, to a library.

"Library" has always seemed to me rather a pretentious word for a collection of two or three thousand books; it has an official and purposeful sound, out of keeping with the casual acquisition of books that one likes and wants to have at hand. Yet there is no escaping the word. Its derivation is impeccable. Its meaning is clear. It is in sanctified usage to cover everything from a few novels in a rental library to the Bodleian and the Widener and the British Museum. If it has connotations that are comprehensive and severe, it has also implications of firelight and close comfort, of gentle study without excessive purpose, of pleasure unbounded by the four walls of any room, always at hand yet reaching out to the ends of the earth and beyond for its inspiration.

Any library, in time, begins to show a purpose. People often ask Ann or me, "How do you go about building a library?" There is no simple answer to that. If you read books and like books well enough to give them space in your house, a library begins to happen to you. And in time it begins to take a rather definite pattern, in direct reflection of your interests. Then you become a shade more conscious about it; you begin to detect gaps in the shelves, even though the books are touching each other, cover to cover; you learn the absorbing delights of the secondhand book catalogues; you detect specialization in yourself and begin to foster it or grow away from it.

A library is many things. It is, first of all, a varied and handsome wall covering with a high insulating value. The books sit on the shelves an average of five or six inches thick, with an air space between themselves and the inner wall; I'm not quite sure what effect the gaps have or the space above the books on each shelf, but I'm sure books keep out some of the cold and heat and I always mean to test it one day with a thermometer.

The cover of every book made since the world began has been a matter of individual thought, and the blending of all this is the calmest, most restful combination of red, blue, green, brown, and gold that ever soothed the senses. I do not think that dust jackets belong on books when they have come to permanent shelves, even though their presence and preservation sometimes have bearing on a book's value. Binders have had such a feeling for moderate color, and massed bindings make such pleasant and rich patterns that it is a pity to disturb them with the sharpness of the jacket designer's more aggressive art.

Books are pleasure, wisdom, experience, emotion, and civilization, and no collection of books that is not rigidly and narrowly specialized can be much less than this. Our own library has shaped itself into six main groups—English literature, which is by far the largest, American literature, Canadian literature, foreign books, reference books, and fishing books. Those are broad headings, but the groups are manageable and one can find one's way easily enough.

Ann had the inspired idea, years ago, that English literature should be arranged by the birth dates of its authors. I was afraid of this at first; I am always suspicious of rearrangements, and Ann's scholarship and erudition are so vastly superior to my own that I visualized her finding her way easily about the shelves while I struggled in confusion and found nothing. Now I wouldn't consider any other arrangement, at least to within fifty years of the present. Those fifteen or twenty shelves are a magnificent parade of history, a firm succession of weighty names whose meaning and effect is clear at a glance. Chaucer, Malory, Bacon, Shakespeare, Donne, Burton; lively Herrick, gentle Walton, giant Milton; the diarists, then Crashaw, Hooker, Defoe, Swift, Addison, Steele, and Pope. So to the first novelists, Richardson, Fielding, Sterne, Smollett. Between Smollett and Jane Austen, at the end of the first section, there is a diversity of giants: Adam Smith, Gibbon, Dr. Johnson, Cobbet of the *Rural Rides*, Blake and Burns before him, Wordsworth, Scott, and Coleridge after.

Such, with slightly lesser names between, is the first section, less than a hundred and fifty volumes, winnowed by time, greatness almost without weakness. It is difficult for me to imagine a library in an English-speaking home without most of them, or without the great Victorians who followed, from Byron and Macaulay down to Hardy and Kipling. There is room for enormous choice between—I find room for White of Selborne, Surtees, Darwin, Hudson, Richard Jefferies; Ann loves Reade and Trollope and the Brontës and has bought them steadily for years; but surely anyone who loves to read must have some of the great names who built the language and the art of writing it.

Beyond the Victorians everything seems current, without the sanctity of age and time. American literature is young, Canadian literature younger still. Yet Whitman and Melville and Hawthorne and Mark Twain clearly belong. Hemingway, Robert Frost, Eugene O'Neill, Stephen Vincent Benét, Sandburg, Dos Passos, Fitzgerald—or do I simply date the time I came to it? Current literature is current literature, and there can be no absolutes. Every reader reads in it, because it is of his time and life. Having read he holds the books or discards them, wisely or unwisely, and no one can know very surely his wisdom or unwisdom. I love American and Canadian literature because they speak directly to me with a fierce urgency and a closeness that is not in things European. American literature is a turbulent, striving present, growing out of massive and enormously diverse creative effort; no one man can keep pace with all the good in its yield and the time of assessment is still far away. The books one keeps on the shelves may be as fine as they seem or they may not. It hardly matters. Even Milton, I suspect, must have flattered some of his contemporaries.

It would be a narrow library that left out foreign books. The greatest of the Russian, French, German, and Italian writers have had such powerful influences on English and American literature that they seem hardly separate from it. If one reads at all one reads them; and because the screen of language is as exclusive as the screen of time these foreigners are great beyond possibility of discard. Who would read Boccaccio or Tolstoy, Proust or Stendhal or Flaubert, and let them go again? They come into a library without being sought and stay there almost on a level with the Greeks and Romans.

I think it would be reasonable to expect most of these things in any library, and they do by themselves make a noble library. But a library that comes into being through the natural growth of reading and keeping books is an intensely personal thing and I know that Ann and I have made some conscious effort to round our few books into a ranging sample of the traditional influences of English writing. This is necessary to us because we live in the country and live by books, and it is necessary again because we are raising children who are intensely curious about the background of their civilization. And it is a choice influenced by many slight chances of education and suggestion throughout our own lives.

Though great literature should be the reason and backbone of any private library, specialization is inevitable and fascinating. We have a shelf of garden books, mostly by Gertrude Jekyll; two or three shelves of natural history, mostly reference books; seven or eight shelves of books about fish and fishing, of every conceivable kind, and two file drawers of pamphlets on fish. The last are mainly my fault, but Ann knows many of them and takes an even stronger interest than I do in the scope and completeness of the collection. There are a dozen or more folio volumes of reproductions of paintings that delight me enormously, modern miracles of printing that match the miracle of the phonograph record. All these things might or might not be in any library. It is only certain that if one does buy and keep books there will be shelves similarly devoted to specialization.

All good books, in a sense, are reference books, and a good library is one that has the answers scattered all through its shelves rather than predigested and collected. But a library needs an atlas and a drawer of local maps. It needs an encyclopedia. It needs a solid dictionary or two. We have those and a scattering of other vague reference books so scrappy and out of date that they should be thrown away.

I have said that a library is many things. It is the beauty of books as well as their substance. When I have been away from home I have remembered many times, without knowing exactly why, the warm red backs of a set of Fielding, the spaced and lovely text of the Nonesuch *Plutarch,* the delicate plates of Ronald's *Flyfisher's Entomology,* the crowded pages of an eighteenth-century Aphra Behn. Ann taught me about fine press books and fine press books have taught me how real is the physical beauty that can be in books. I had thought once that one should only ask of a book that the text be complete and readable; there had seemed a measure of emptiness in admiring a fine binding or a handsome make-up. But there is real happiness in such things because the bookmaker's art is a real art; it cannot add to the magic of great words, but it can put them in worthy setting and contribute in a strange, self-effacing way some new dimension to the pleasure of reading. Collecting fine press books is no hobby for a poor man, yet I think a few fine press books belong in every library as a reminder of skills perfectly blended into a single art—the skill of the papermaker and type founder, the printer and binder and decorator. In ambitious moments I should like to own an example of every major fine press; yet I am happy enough with those we have—half a dozen Nonesuch books, a lovely Golden Cockerel printed blacker than black on whitest of white, some Derrydales, a Grabhorn, a single Kelmscott, and a score or more of other books whose perfection is such that one returns again and again to take them down and turn the pages.

I think a library should not be a static thing but rather like a deep pool in a river, whose depths move slowly if at all but whose surface is a quiet flow. Fresh books come in, others are moved on the shelves to make place for them, others again go on to their travels through the secondhand dealers. Never sell a book, only take a credit and find another book to replace it, sometimes two to replace one, sometimes one to replace half a dozen. Books are never really bought and sold, only leased for a lifetime, on deposit, or perhaps two lifetimes. In the end they will go back to the dealers, out again and back again until some have served successive leaseholders through three or four hundred years, as have some of the books in this room.

People who come into this room sometimes ask in wonder, "Have you read all these books?" There couldn't be a more reasonable question, or a more natural answer than "No." Yet I always feel that I have betrayed the questioner when I say no; he seemed so certain that the answer would be yes, that he would be able to see with his own eyes the head that held such a wealth of knowledge. I sometimes admit to myself now, cautiously and reluctantly, there are books here that I shall never read, and still others, read and well loved, that I may never read again. But so long as they are here, within reach, there is always the possibility that the mood or the need or the time will come when I shall read quietly and completely through the whole of the *Anatomy of Melancholy* or North's *Plutarch*, when I shall turn again to *War and Peace* or *Kristin Lavransdatter*.

One other question, still more flattering, almost as hard to answer negatively, is, "Did you write all these books?" When an adult asks me, I can shake my head and point to the one little shelf with its ten titles in some thirty editions, and still hold a measure of self-respect. But when one of my children's friends asks and I have to say no, I feel I have destroyed a faith that can never grow again.

NOVEMBER

THE FALSE ACACIAS AND THE walnuts are among the last trees to put out leaves in the spring and the last to lose them in the fall. But their ways are very different. The walnuts are stripped almost bare in a single night of frost, the leaves cut away into a pile of black and brown around the base of the tree. It is a minor, seasonal emergency to collect the nuts for the kitchen, then rake the leaves and move them away to mulch the rhododendrons before their sodden, bitter weight can spoil the grass of the lawn. There is something in the harsh, clear smell of those leaves that I find emotionally stirring and I wonder each year if it is valid or imagined. Once I confused the stain of walnut juice with woad and thought I had made a discovery, then remembered that we as children used to mark ourselves with the green hulls of walnuts and call it woad. Perhaps I had made the discovery, at that; back thirty years instead of three thousand.

The false acacia leaves fall singly and unaccountably on even the stillest November days, plummeting down with a determination that seems out of all proportion to their weight. Like alder leaves, they fall green and are flat on the ground when they have fallen, not rustling and shriveled and curled as are the maple leaves. I think of acacia leaves falling this way as a white mist comes windlessly along the river from the sea, with the gulls crying in it and flying down through it, magnified to the size of eagles.

The river is full of gulls in November, because the salmon are dying. Generally I do not find them interesting or too attractive. They fly beautifully and swim gracefully, but they are primarily scavengers and spend most of their time waiting with receptive dignity until the river brings a dead fish and they turn suddenly to clumsy, pointless quarreling among themselves, often allowing something just as good to drift by unnoticed. And occasionally they attack a salmon that is still living. There isn't a reason in nature why they shouldn't; the fish is dying, exhausted and helpless, drifting or swimming weakly near the surface, his protective coloring long since destroyed by the contrast of white fungus patches against the dark pigmentation of spawning. He has no conceivable chance to go on living and by the time they plunge their vicious, blood-spotted beaks at him he is probably beyond fear; but I am still sentimentalist enough to feel that a spawned-out salmon should die in peace or else in some more sudden way.

Now the same sentimental concern has interested me in a gull. For the last three days a big gull has been industriously washing himself over on the far side of the river. There is a great black patch of oil on his breast and he seems to hope that fresh water and hard work will clear it away; if he is wrong, I suppose he will die, and his industry and determination suggest that he thinks the same. Yet he is not hurried or frantic or undignified, but somehow calmer and more confident than the other gulls. He stands in the water for five or ten minutes at a time, plunging his head and breast down violently into it, preening a little, occasionally flapping his wings, sometimes pausing to look around with the careful, all-seeing head movements of an eagle perched on a snag. Then he climbs onto a rock and stands preening vigorously for several minutes, until it is time to go back into the water. He can fly well and seems able to compete. Other gulls sit around on rocks sunning themselves while he works, but when a piece of salmon drifts down the river and stirs them he flies with the rest and often wins out in the mewing, flapping struggle. It almost seems as though the others are a little awed and respectful; they slide off their rocks when he lands beside them and are less determined in struggling for food with him than among themselves. Yesterday one seemed to be helping him with the oil for quite a long while, standing near him in the water and sometimes plucking at his breast with its beak. I want the big gull to get himself clean and survive because his calm perseverance seems admirable. Whether or not I like gulls, and I am still doubtful, I know I hate oil.

It was easy to watch the salmon in the low water of this year's early November and as usual I watched them, going out in a canoe to hold onto the pole against the swift water when their splashings and excitements stirred my curiosity too much. About fifty yards below the big rock on the far side, where the eddy had closed in on itself and the current began to draw smoothly and strongly again, there were always a hundred or more of them in various stages of spawning. I saw them as light and dark shapes against the rocky bottom, sometimes marked out by the white of fungus patches or worn tails, but all strong fish still, able to hold their depth and place in the stream; the weaker fish were beyond them, in the shallower water near the bank, and their feebleness showed in the frequent lazy breaking of frayed tails and bony dorsal fins above the surface. The strong fish were a mixed group, springs and cohos and dog salmon for the most part, but a few of them late humpbacks. A few were still spawning, the females turning on their sides to dig away the gravel, the males restless nearby; but most seemed to be waiting, just holding there to let the swift water wash by them, occasionally forcing against it in sudden fear or impatience, perhaps searching for more oxygen than the water would readily give them, perhaps stirred by some warning weakness of decaying muscles.

In the eddy behind the big rock there were only a few fish, cohos as nearly as I could tell and strong, not weak and searching shelter as I had expected. A little above the rock was a single big spring salmon, a male of fifty pounds or more. He was through spawning and badly worn, but he seemed to be holding very easily in the strong water, drifting across a few feet, then back into place again. Occasionally he made a little drive against the current, only to let himself drift back; quite often his dorsal fin broke the surface of the water and sometimes he seemed not to care, sometimes he forced himself back down to the bottom again. His mouth opened and closed steadily, almost rhythmically, but with a lifting of his head that seemed strained and gulping.

Fifty yards above him two beautiful silvery females were dead on the bottom of the river. I stirred them with the canoe pole and judged from their swollen vents and frayed tails that they had probably spawned successfully; yet it seemed strange they should be dead when far more cruelly scarred and battered fish were living.

In the center of the stream, under the rapid, I could see no fish, and there were only a few dark cohos among the big rocks on this side. I let the canoe drift back to the landing and stirred a migrating flock of pine siskins from the alder by the ramp. These are November birds, repeating themselves faithfully year after year, hanging like little brown leaves all over the alder tree to work at the catkins, wheeling suddenly from there clear across the river, sweeping into another tree on the far side, leaving that after two or three minutes to loop and twist and dip their way back to the Balm of Gilead, the whole flock of two or three hundred so matched in mood that scarcely a wing beat separates them at any time.

Now that I have written of salmon and gulls I remember that I watched two gulls with a dead salmon in the November after V-J Day. It was a day of southeast storm, wild and wet, but the gulls were sheltered from the storm at the edge of a rising, clouded stream, standing on a sandbar, pulling at the salmon carcass, absorbed, safe, important. I had and still have a vivid impression of the feet and legs of the gulls (bright orange it seemed to me, though gulls do not have bright orange feet and legs) against the grey sandbar. It seemed the first clear and simple thing I had noticed for many years. Walking, there had been no sky overhead to look into, no real earth underfoot, nothing about to be seen for the simple sake of seeing and feeling. One had groped through an intense fog of absorption, always a little afraid of being lost, ashamed of being distracted. The gulls with their salmon broke through that grey absorption, themselves grey and white on a grey day with the grey carcass of the salmon against grey sand. But there were the impossible orange feet. A symbol of release or else a warning to observe more closely.

ON WOOD

A FEW YEARS AGO WE USED TO cut about twenty cords of wood and pile it into the basement every fall. It was alder for the most part, cut from the stand on the far side of the road, long straight trees up to eighteen inches or so on the stump and clean of limbs for fifty or sixty feet of their height. Felled in spring and summer, cut into four-foot lengths and split once, then piled, the wood was perfectly seasoned for burning by fall. Left in the round or over a winter, the heart goes out of it and it becomes soft and half rotten, with only a fraction of its heat left in it.

Reg cut his own needs from his own alder patch in the same way and we got together each fall to cut the cordwood into stove wood and haul it in. He had rigged an old Star motor on a sled to drive a circular saw by a long belt; a forty-five-gallon oil drum fed the cooling system and the rig was good, though temperamental sometimes. We were all temperamental, Reg and myself and Joe, who usually came to help, and old Bill, the big horse that hauled the sled from place to place. We would get together as soon as it seemed decent to take a few days out from hunting, which was always much later than it should have been, and fly at the business with a terrific urgency compounded of guilty consciences and the daily sterner signs of approaching bad weather. The Star motor would usually balk a little at starting after its long layoff; there was always some adjusting to be done before the opposed pulleys were well enough in line to hold the belt, but in the end the belt would stay on, the motor would pick up speed, and the saw would begin to hum, then whine until it was at just the right note—and we would start.

It was my job to feed the saw from the cordwood pile, swinging the wood onto the table and sliding it through until it came under Reg's hands at the right length for the saw. Then Reg would tilt the table into the saw and Joe would flip the block away as it came free. We all wanted to be through with the job and away to our other affairs, so we kept at it steadily, moving the saw as seldom as possible so as not to tempt the pulleys out of line again or give the Star an unnecessary chance to be difficult. Sometimes we would get a run of two or more hours at a stretch with everything going smoothly and I would be packing cordwood six or eight steps before we decided to cut the motor and move. At other times the belt would slip or the Star would speed up or slow down or the saw frame would have to be adjusted on the sled, and we would all solemnly swear and work away until everything was running again. When we finally had to move the rig there would be the ceremony of hitching old Bill and arguing him into the mighty heave he had to make to get the sled moving, then, almost in the same breath, into stopping again before he was off with it beyond the end of the pile. It was a fine time and we liked it and hated it and enjoyed each other all the while, Reg intent and urgent, worrying about his machine, Joe calm and joking always, myself untidy and torn and sweating, with gloves worn through by the end of the second spell.

The old urgency has gone from getting in the wood now that we burn oil in the kitchen stove and coal in the furnace, and it's hard to remember how much work it was and how important. Even after it had been pitched from the piles in the field into the truck, from the truck into the basement, there was still the job of piling inside the basement to make room for it all, rows and rows and rows that filled nearly the whole of the thirty-by-forty-foot space and would all be gone within twelve months, split again, piled into woodboxes, lifted at last into stoves and fireplaces. Now there is just enough of it to recapture the old sensations and, strangely, they are all good.

Up north, before I was married, we used to go out and beachcomb logs, preferably fir, on the salt water, tow them up the river, and beach them with jacks at high tide. If we were lucky we borrowed a drag saw to cut the stove blocks, otherwise we swung for days on the end of a cross-cut. Then we loaded the blocks on a sled and persuaded Tony, the big white ox, to haul them up to the house; there we split them to stove wood in an outside woodshed, piled it full, and packed armloads twice a day through the dairy and larder to fill the kitchen woodbox. An enormous labor and repetition of labor, yet it seemed to leave us more time to do the things we wanted than there is now. And no one underrated a full woodshed; it was a sign of proficient and forehanded men, as surely as the buck hanging from the gambrel and the fish piled in the smokehouse.

We used sometimes to pack in wood—"logs," we called it —for grandfather's fire from a great scented basket lined with green baize in the passage outside his door. He would handle the pieces lovingly, asking us to recognize sycamore from elm, beech from ash, showing us how each wood burned and warning us that it was always sinful waste to burn coal and wood together. I now think coal and wood together make one of the pleasantest fires there is and by no means an outrageously extravagant one; but I still love the different burning qualities of different woods and am always squirreling away some special wood for a special evening's burning. Often I envy the Easterner his varied hardwoods.

November

Here on the Pacific Coast our abundant natives are Douglas fir, western hemlock, red cedar, amabilis fir, Sitka spruce, maple, and alder. Douglas fir is the most commonly used firewood and it is a worthy wood, easy to dry, straight-splitting, burning with a fine and generous heat so long as it has plenty of oxygen—not a wood to smolder and glow and hold in, but fine for stoves and a cheerful flaming fire. The bark is even better fuel than the wood itself. Often three or four inches thick, creviced and corky, blacksmiths have told me it will make a welding heat in the right fire. I burned it for years in the heavy timber, stripping the dry undersides of leaning trees —it flakes away under the axe in great slabs—laying a single slab flat on the ground, shaving pitchwood onto it, then building a circle of lesser slabs into a foot-high cylinder around the flaming pitch. When the small fire had boiled water and cooked supper it was hot enough to make the foundation for a larger fire of inferior fuel. I still look at a big leaning fir in the woods with an appraising eye, judging whether the bark of the underside is hard or soft, thin or thick, easy to flake away or clinging closely. I doubt if woodsmen anywhere in the world have quicker and surer, more generous native fuel.

Hemlock is hard to season, but burns honestly and cleanly with a good heat when fully dry. Red cedar is quick and hot, splits out sliver thin at the touch of an axe, and makes perfect kindling. It dries readily, is proof against rot for years, has a lovely color and scent. But it will not last in a fire and it burns with a fierce sputtery crackling that no man wants for longer than the start of his fire. Spruce and the true firs burn away quickly, without much heat; a woodpile of either is a false show, put up by an ignorant or improvident man unless it is wood he has to be rid of. Alder, properly seasoned, is a noble wood, full of heat, free of sparks and all uncertainty; but it burns away too quickly for perfection. Of all our coast woods only the broadleaf maple is perfect, a calm hot wood that burns slowly and steadily, often with blue flames of its own gases, never throwing sparks, never sealing itself away in carbon, glowing with heat to the end. But maple is too seldom an easy wood to get. It grows scattered and we prize the trees too much to cut them easily. Nor is it an easy tree to cut into wood, because it usually splits into separate trunks or heavy limbs only a few feet from the ground. We are used to the tall straight trees of the true forest and hesitate before the gnarled and twisty mass of a great maple. Perhaps it's just as well. Better the live tree standing than the finest fuel in the world so long as there is other to be had.

I have never tried to burn the broadleaf maple green in the woods, but its tiny cousin, the vine maple, is the best of all fuels in the mountain country. It grows beautifully in long, slender trunks, the largest only a few inches in diameter, which sprawl over the mountain flats under the timber in such delicate patterns that one hates to cut it at all. I usually hunt out a cluster of trunks growing more nearly upright and cut out the straightest of them. The wood cuts cleanly under a sharp axe for all its density, and splits cleanly through its length. I start a fire of dry cedar, then stand the green-barked lengths of vine maple around it in a pyramid. They catch quickly and burn quietly, with a fine heat in spite of their greenness—because of it, I suppose, since there must be some quality of burning in the sap and life of the tree, some chemical formation that releases gases to make the quick blue flame. If one has to cook in the open, this is the best and cleanest cooking fire I know.

I often wonder what kind of a mind it is that enjoys splitting wood. I can do it happily for hours, given a splitting block of the right height and my own short-handled four-pound splitting axe. I think busily of many things and often of the wood itself. Every block has character. The stove blocks are straight and clear and dull; they split away cleanly and easily in a rhythm of sound that is yield without effort. It is relief to come upon a twisted, malformed monster and puzzle a way between the knots, across them or even through them. This is fireplace wood, better for it than any more standard yield of the tree; some of the knots are so distinctive that one remembers them all the way from the tree to wood-box and fireplace and watches them burn with greater satis-faction for that. I remember one old farmer who got caught by the kickback of a twisty, pitch-seamed fir one fall and broke several ribs. He swore through the rest of the winter he could recognize every stick that came from that tree and as he picked one up for the fire he would say, "That's the son of a bitch that put me in hospital last fall." And there was Andy, the trapper at Claire Lake, who chopped off his thumb as he was splitting a knot one winter, then kept the knot and the thumb until he could invite several of us in to witness the burning of both with proper ceremony. "Any bastardly chunk that can trick me out of a thumb has got a cremation coming to it," Andy told us. "And a wake too. We'll open a couple of crocks."

I split coal as well as wood now and that also is a minor art. I think I understand wood, but coal I do not. Sometimes a single gentle blow shatters a piece to dust; sometimes a minute of vicious hammering seems to get nowhere; as often as not a lump splits exactly the way I don't expect it to, across the grain when I'm striking for along, along when I'm trying for across. I know enough now to suspect anything that looks too smooth and flat; as likely as not it's limestone and a good sharp tap sends the chips flying everywhere. I know enough to start with gentle treatment, scarcely more than the ham-

mer's own weight in falling, and watch for a crack. I can follow up an advantage like that and make the most of it. But I
shall never split coal without remembering the comment of
Buster, my long-suffering partner of many years ago. We
were living in a small gas boat at the time and burning coal in
the cookstove. I went up on deck and tackled a large lump
with the dogging hammer. I hit it at the end, in the middle,
on both sides, turned it, tried again. Minor chips flew about
all over the deck and battered against the pilothouse door, but
the main lump changed little in size or character. Then Buster
came up from below. "My God," he said. "Don't you know
anything? You come from the greatest coal-producing nation
in the world and you can't even split the darn stuff."

He took the hammer, rolled the lump once, and demolished
it with half a dozen scientific taps. "You just have to figure
it out a bit," he said. "That's all." I'm still figuring. But it is
difficult to imagine anyone born in British Columbia who
wouldn't know how to split wood.

ON HUNTING

I HAVE HUNTED ALL MY LIFE AND
loved hunting deeply, from the earliest days of stalking sparrows and occasional rabbits with an air rifle to the search for
goats in the high mountains and the problems of wild geese
on the flats. I still love hunting as a supreme sport, infinitely
more challenging and exciting than any of the artificial con-
tests between men that are commonly called sport. But I have
realized, and admitted to myself at last, that I don't like killing; that I never did like it.

November

For a keen hunter, that is an admission close to schizophrenia, yet it really makes sense; hunting and killing are two different things. The joy and satisfaction of hunting is alive in every movement up to the shot. With the shot it dies, almost as surely as the creature dies. If one does not shoot, everything goes on.

I have not learned this easily or suddenly, or, as yet, completely. I realize now that the thought was always somewhere in me because there have always been times when, a little ashamedly because it was against my training, I would disregard a perfectly satisfactory shot. But the first time I admitted it to myself was at the edge of a frost-bound swamp where I set the sights on the shaggy neck of a great bull elk; he had just raised his head to the sun, not seventy-five yards from me, and I lowered the rifle because he was too beautiful not to see with normal eyes. I raised it again and held the sights steady on a perfect neck shot, just to show I could do it; but I knew he was too much life and too much grandeur for me to kill.

In the years before I wrote the book *Ki-yu* I hunted and killed a fair number of cougars. Cougars are predators, the government pays a bounty on them, and I was working honestly enough to learn as much as I possibly could about them; but after the excitement and interest of the first two or three I always hated the moment of the shot. Once or twice I have taken the dogs from under a tree without shooting and this seems at first the perfect solution; but it is something one can do only in very remote and unsettled country, where there are no other hunters, because a cougar that has become used to dogs is likely to turn on them and kill them. Cougar hunting is immeasurably the most interesting form of large-game hunting I have known, the strongest test of a man's woodcraft and endurance, calling for truly beautiful work by well-trained dogs; cougars have to be kept in some measure of control in a settled country, so I have no doubt I shall hunt them again. But I shall never come to the kill without reluctance.

It is still an illogical position, built from emotion, not logic. I like the doctrine that all life is sacred, that nothing should be killed; some religions have professed it and gone to great lengths to observe it, but it is an absurdity; man could not have survived or developed under it, and he could not now survive for long if he attempted to observe it. One cannot walk without sometimes killing ants or beetles or other small creatures; one cannot grow crops without insecticides or dig in the earth without crushing things or even maintain human health without killing rats and flies and lice. One kills to eat unless one is a vegetarian and kills for clothing and kills for learning. In all these killings there is a satisfying purpose, clear to most people and beyond argument.

Once there was a similar purpose in hunting. Man hunted and killed for food. On the North American continent today, south of the Arctic circle, man hunts for sport, not food. And now that hunting is one of the most widely followed of all sports it cannot be otherwise; there is enough game only if men hunt for sport and kill sparingly. The pleasure of hunting is, I believe, a perfectly legitimate purpose. It is a compound pleasure, deeply emotional, set in a valid tradition; it increases a man by teaching him constantly more of his world, by bringing him against stronger truths than most to be found in the day-to-day routine of civilized living. Hunting takes men where they would not otherwise go, shows them creatures they would not otherwise see. It builds warm companionship and strong friendships. It leaves a man with memories that are among the richest of his whole life. These are not trivial matters. They are a whole lot less trivial, I suspect, than a mink coat or a cashmere sweater or even a filet mignon. They do not, or should not, grow out of killing, but out of hunting.

I had supposed, at one stage, that I had resolved the matter for myself, found a sensible dividing line I could cling to. When I moved down from the north and admitted the existence of butcher shops, it was no longer a part of living to kill deer for food. I admitted this with a sense of relief and admitted at the same time that I never wanted to kill another bear, another goat, another cougar, large game of any kind. The rifle, the calm shot, a weight of death greater than my own weight, were not for me. But the shotgun, the swift wingshot, the intricate work of good dogs, the hard walking over the long hills, and among the rustling leaves and frost-browned grasses of the quiet places in the old logging works, were something else again. I did not want to shoot limits or kill easily. I wanted only to get out, to watch my dogs work closely, keenly, wisely in the skills they were bred to. I wanted to find often enough and kill often enough for this, and to hold sometimes in my hand the lovely pattern of feathers and colors that is a freshly killed ruffed grouse. This I did and was satisfied for a while, calm in my mind, rewarded by all the pleasures a hunter should know and a greater intensity in them because the intensity of my hunting was less. Such destruction as I wrought was insignificant, far less than that of the winter to come, or the cycle to come; my kills were scattered over a wide area, never grouped in a single covey; and I compensated when I could by killing occasional crows and accipitrine hawks and domestic cats gone wild. There seemed reason and a safe moderation in my sport that diminished nothing, yet increased many things for me and the friends with whom I hunted.

But the progressive admission of my own unfitness to be a

hunter goes on. I hunt as often as I can get out, with greater enthusiasm and interest than ever; I shoot less and less, and with an ever-increasing reluctance, because a wholly new factor has come in to destroy all the calculations that once seemed to make my measure of killing reasonable and sane: I am no longer a single hunter among a few others of my kind; I am part of a vast and always increasing army of hunters that suddenly seems to threaten the future of every wild creature I love. The continent is opened now, reached and covered. Industry and other development crowds hunter and hunted into narrower and narrower space. As the space narrows and the breeding and spread of the creatures are steadily reduced, the army of hunters steadily increases. It blankets every flyway, combs every thicket and woodland and field and plain. And it is overwhelmingly an army whose sport is killing, not hunting; whose gods are ballistics and bag limits and cold-storage lockers instead of the careful work of dogs, the mysteries of flight lines and cover, the smell of the fall woods and the feel of natural ground underfoot; whose transportation is the automobile whenever and wherever possible. I do not think there is room for much killing of mine in all this. My thought is rather to spare and save and hope and, when I do hunt to kill, to go as far afield as I can.

I do not mean by this that the end is tomorrow or the next day, only that the way of it is clear. It is the way of the trumpeter swan and the heath hen, the wild turkey and the passenger pigeon, the ivory-billed woodpecker, the buffalo, the mountain sheep. I realize that not all these creatures are extinct, that there is real hope some of them may grow back into reasonable abundance. But I do not care to think that creatures we now reckon abundant, part of the delight of every man's eyes in his daily living, may be reduced and driven back to the limits of parks and sanctuaries. I would rather not kill at all if it means that my grandson will never watch a flight of wild geese against the sky, will never see a black bear wheel in smoothest motion to his scent, will never know the thrill of pintails riding in to settle.

Years ago, when I was hunting geese along a chain of lakes and swamps, I heard a party of deer hunters fire several shots a mile or so away from me. I went over to the sound and found a little lake with three dead swans floating on its surface. There was no sign of the hunters and it was a still day, so I swam out and brought in the swans. They had been killed by rifles, for "sport" presumably, though they were protected birds even at that time. Less than a month ago a friend of mine was fishing in a lake when a lone swan lit not far from him. Almost at once two men pushed off from shore in a power boat, came near the swan and shot at it with a rifle. It was wounded, so they chased it with the power boat, caught it, dragged it in and killed it. The swan was protected by law from hunting of any kind; all migratory birds are protected from hunters with rifles or in power boats. But the swan is dead. Multiply this by all the thousands of brutal, thoughtless, ignorant individuals who carry firearms in the name of "sport" and it is easy to see why a residue of five hundred or a thousand trumpeter swans may be too few to perpetuate themselves in spite of all the protection they can be given.

Remember the thousands upon thousands of hunters to whom hunting is shooting and everything between shots is slow. Remember how many men believe that a bag limit, preferably in competition with their fellows, is high triumph. Remember the hunters who overshoot limits, who fail to pick up birds they have killed and shoot others instead, who wound more birds than they ever bring home. Remember that the number and proportion of all these increases steadily year by year, that new roads open up new country, that settlement and development closes older country, and I think the pattern is clear. There cannot be stocks of wild life to maintain the sport indefinitely.

Yet sportsmen, hunters and fishermen are the keenest and most effective of all conservationists. If they are responsible for nine-tenths of the avoidable destruction of wildlife, they are responsible for at least nine-tenths of the effective conservation, because they have the numbers and organization and voting weight to be effective, and because they have the strongest of all possible reasons to be effective: their own survival as hunters is exactly related to the survival of the creatures they hunt. Many do not see this clearly or, seeing it, do not care. But many have worked and are working militantly and wisely and creatively to save and build. The hardest task they have to do is to persuade their fellow hunters that sport is hunting, not killing.

Some of my friends ask me why, if I feel all this so strongly, I have not long ago turned from the gun to the camera. The answer is that I want to see everything with my eyes, in the field, to be as free as possible to see and yet keyed to keenest perception. A camera seems an intolerable impediment to all this. I have never known a camera hunter who did not become a fanatic, deeply involved by the technical and mechanical aspects of his sport, limited by weather and light and an enormous weight and bulk of gear. His rewards are great; he captures much of the beauty of flight and movement and country, he captures color and light and even some things that are too quick for the eye to see; and he can live all this over again not once but many times from his easy chair by the fire. But these are not the rewards I want. I want all the senses free, I want the full flash of beauty and incident from normal eye to mind and heart. Even the gun sometimes interferes with this, though far more often it sharpens and concentrates the senses. If I ever do leave the gun aside it will be for a pair of high-grade binoculars, not a camera.

But I like the gun. It is a familiar thing, full of associations. I am a different man when I am carrying it, more alert, more careful, more purposeful than without it. Carrying a gun has taught me a thousand things about animals and country and wind and weather that I should not otherwise have bothered to learn, has taken me to a thousand places I should not otherwise have seen. I still like the excitement of the quick snap shot among brush and trees, of waiting as wild fowl wheel into range, of planning and stalking, anticipating flight or rise. Killing has a place in hunting, if only a small one. I see it as a rite, a sacrifice, an acknowledgment of the sport's origin that gives meaning to what has gone before. But never as an end in itself.

The test of all this will be in my son, Alan. He is eight years old now, growing up in a country where every man and boy is interested in guns and hunting, and he is already interested. Remembering what the gun has taught me, the pleasure it has given me, the intensity of devotion it has called from me, I cannot in honesty deny him the same things, nor could I hope to be effective if I did so.

But his introduction to it all is different from mine. I learned about snipe, for instance, from hunting; saw my first snipe with a gun in my hands, learned the likeliest places to look for them, learned to walk down wind on them because they hold better that way, hesitating to rise with a wind behind them; I learned their lines of passage from place to place because I had a gunner's interest, learned the manner of their sharp rise from swampy ground, solved the quick twistings of their early flight, reacted so often to their scraping cry that I still cannot hear it without swift response in the muscles of my arms and shoulders. And, still because I was a gunner, I could not leave them alone in the closed season but went out in the swamps to hear their drumming at mating time, watching the lovely flight and the sharp dive with spread tail feathers that made the sound. And later I learned to find occasional nests, built at the end of long tunnels of swamp grass. All these things are immensely precious to me, though I rarely hunt snipe now. But I should not have learned them if I had not been a hunter.

The Wilson's snipe come to our own fields here first in October. They seem tame then yet cautious, hunting over the high ground among dead bracken and thistles. They fly a little way, pitch and, if you are still, stand up quite boldly, long bills poised, heads cocked, handsome orange-red tails brilliant as those of ruffed grouse. Later they are always in the swampy ground along the edge of the alders. Alan and I go out sometimes to find them, walking quietly down wind, without guns, hoping that one of us will be quick enough to see a bird on the ground before it jumps in a quick little thunder of wings to flash away among the trees. We rarely do. I try to tell him about the excitement and problems of hunting them and I wonder if he can feel the same thrill from the bird as I do or whether for him it is another and better thrill or just a bird, no more and no less worth seeing than a song sparrow or a junco.

Whatever his satisfactions, he is already a good observer; and for all his talk of guns and shootings he is a most reluctant killer. A friend gave him a humane trap last year and from time to time he sets it and catches barn rats. I gently suggest they would be well out of the way, preferably drowned. But he takes them across the creek and releases them there to go about their evil business. It is a fortunate reluctance, for his inheritance is less than mine was. He will, if he is lucky, start hunting ducks with a six-weeks' season and a six- or eight-bird limit; I started with a three-months' season and a twenty-four-bird limit. He may, again if he is lucky, know an open ruffed grouse season here on Vancouver Island; there was a time not long ago when the October days in search of ruffed grouse were the peak days of the season for me. Yet there will, I think, be all the hunting he wants and a chance of more killing than he needs. If he remains reluctant, if he approaches killing with respect and understanding, if he is a hunter, not a butcher, there should still be enough for his son and his grandson after him.

DECEMBER

Our expected cold is in January and February. December is wet for the most part, alternations of frost and heavy, rain-filled gales from the southeast. But this year the steady cold has come early; there has been snow on the ground since the first of the month, night after night has been silent and gleaming with frost and there has been little thawing through the days.

Two days ago, after coming back from school, Alan went off on some affairs of his own on the other side of the river and towards dark it seemed necessary to go and look for him. It was a clear evening after a clear day, and a strongish west breeze had started as the sun set. A brand new sliver of moon was low in the southern sky and without thinking, still walking steadily, I bowed to it three times and turned the money in my pocket. Not, of course, that I'm superstitious. Bowing to the new moon is just a countryman's courtesy, natural as breathing. And groping for the money in the pocket, wondering whether it should be turned three times or only once or the more times the better—that's just a tribute to a quaint tradition, a generous identification of my most sophisticated self with simple people who have done the same thing for thousands of years back. It is always encouraging, too, to find the money there; the amount doesn't matter, a few coppers are every bit as good as a handful of silver dollars; better probably, because the increase is more obviously due.

I knew by this time, having passed his nearer haunts, that I could expect to walk for another mile or more before I found Alan. I thought of how often I had seen the new moon with nothing in my pocket to turn. That always seems bad for a moment, yet one's excuses are always excellent; in the woods, where one doesn't use money, why carry it? Or what better excuse could there be for not carrying money than having none to carry? And where is the virtue in carrying money if one has it? The important thing is to recognize the moon and remember the business about turning the money; any reasonable moon must surely take the will for the deed and recognize an empty pocket as the perfect subject for increase, even though twice or thrice zero is still zero to a mathematician.

All this is just tolerant concession to old-fashioned whimsey, of course. I don't plant potatoes, or dig them, in the dark of the moon; not knowingly, I mean. I do argue with Ann that weather often changes on the full moon and am powerfully supported in this by Uncle Reg; Ann would have won the argument long ago, but we are pretty shifty in it and so is the weather, so Reg and I still cling to a few shreds of conviction. And I'd as soon not see a new moon for the first time through glass. That's very bad, they say. One can rationalize it; obviously a countryman should be outdoors at the time of a clear evening when the new moon shows; if not he's probably sick or not tending his business well enough to prosper. Just the same, I'd prefer not to see it through glass.

I saw Alan walking the road towards me, his small, straight

body dark against the snow banks. He began to run. The trouble with all the rationalization, I thought, is the emotion one feels at every sight of the moon, especially the new moon. The sense of gratitude, of affinity, of friendly awe. I bow in gratitude, turn the money in expectation. Not that the money will be doubled, or that the moon will damn my agriculture or my fishing or my books if I miss one bow. But a man expects at each new phase of anything; even the intellectual allows himself expectations of a new century, even practical souls use decades to measure their memories and justify their hopes; and the common man, whether he shines shoes or runs a bank, expects something of each new year. So the countryman recognizes that something of his fate is marked by the moon's sliver, whether it is the lambing moon or the sowing moon, the hunting moon or the harvest moon. Being a man, he hopes that it will be good and likes to record his hope.

Alan reached me, a little breathlessly. "Did you see the moon, Daddy? It's only just starting, but it's nearly as bright as day."

Children really shouldn't be allowed to exaggerate without some sort of check. "Well," I said. "It's not really all that bright. The snow helps a lot."

Last night was cloudy and snowing a little, but there was light from the moon behind the clouds. Primrose did not come in for her hay and grain at milking time and she still had not been in to the barn at ten o'clock, so I took the lantern and went to follow her tracks through the alders. Near the creek I came suddenly upon a splash of blood in the snow and found a freshly killed coho salmon. It was a male, a handsome red fish still in good condition. One eye had been torn out, there was a deep bite in the belly, near the pectoral fins, and another at the back of the neck. As I looked at him his gill-covers opened and closed twice.

The old snow was frozen hard and the new snow was only a scattering in there under the trees, but I knew I should be able to see a bear track if there was one. I searched for several yards on either side of the fish and found nothing. The creek was flowing gently, five or six feet wide at this point and some eighteen inches deep. I could not see that the ice along its edges had been disturbed or find any clear track of blood between the water and where the fish lay, two or three yards from the bank. I did not think an otter would come to such a place. No eagle would fly at night. So far as I know even the great snowy owl, which I have seen several times back in the alders, does not hunt fish. It had to be mink or coon or cat, yet I could not believe any of these could handle a strong eight- or ten-pound fish and leave so little trace of struggle. I turned the lantern on the trees and found him almost at once, right at the top of a tall slim willow: a tiny coon, no more than half-grown. That didn't satisfy me at all, so I searched other trees, all the nearby trees, expecting to find larger coons, but I found nothing.

Because it seemed intensely dramatic and still something of a mystery I hurried back to the house to fetch Ann. We came back to the place cautiously and I shone the light towards the fish at the last possible moment. The little coon ran away from it, over to a small spruce tree, and began to climb. There was no other coon, no other sign of life at all. We followed him and watched him climb, pausing often to look down at us, wary but not afraid. He had eaten a little more from his big fish while I was over at the house, so we left him to it and followed Primrose's tracks until they brought us out to the pasture again and we saw her in the faint light, moving massively against the snow.

December

This morning, with light snow still falling, I went back to the creek again. There was no sign of the fish except blood under the new snow and a single clot of blood on the far side of the creek. The snow had covered whatever tracks there might have been and I could not tell certainly whether the fish had been dragged away or torn up and eaten. Three mallards flew out of the creek as I searched and a heron squawked and lumbered away from near the fence line. At the edge of the pasture a snipe flew up, straight up until he was clear of the treetops, then along. A lot goes on over in the alders.

SALT WATER AND TIDEFLATS

EVEN LIVING ON AN ISLAND, ONE becomes very much land-bound by the habit of the road and the automobile. Travel by boat is slow and precarious, always at the control of tides and weather, and a power boat of any size is a lot to worry about when one is not using it. A car sits safely waiting, is always ready to go, and makes good time in almost any weather; ferries carry it safely and comfortably to the mainland and the roads of a continent.

Yet I miss boats and the sea, the challenge of weather, the friendship of little harbors, the particular sense of freedom and reach that boats give. In the north we had nothing but boats or our feet; a seven-knot boat was fast compared to walking, it opened up a lot of new country, and it was luxuriously comfortable if it had a cabin and pilothouse. I have never liked power boats for their own sake, any more than I like automobiles or airplanes or guns for their own sake. But they are a way to wonderful things.

The thing I miss most is the sense of intimacy with the sea—not the wide sea, but the narrow coastwise seas, the channels and inlets and bays, the urgent tides, the varied, complicated shores. It still seems strange to hear a gale blowing up and not be concerned, to study the tide book only once or twice a month instead of daily, to watch the coming and going of small boats with a sense of detachment instead of intimate concern. In the north we fetched our mail by boat and all the food we bought, we went visiting by boat, often running from dawn to dark to get to a Saturday night dance, and we used boats in our work, hand-logging or fishing, even for some of our trap lines.

There were many boats, of many kinds. Once Ed and I had nothing better than a water-logged Peterborough canoe, but we crossed Johnstone Strait in it twice a week through a whole winter and never missed a mail day until the police stopped us in March. I think that was the closest intimacy with the sea I have ever had; in the trough of the wave from a good southeast gale we would see only water, angry and twisted and breaking; then the canoe would rise on the next swell, up and up until we could see the land ahead and the land behind; and the combers broke, hissing and splattering spray after us, only a foot or two from Ed's hand on the stern paddle. One had a sense of wading through the sea as through heavy wet brush, except that it was easier and more exciting; the only water we shipped was spindrift from the whitecaps and the canoe seemed able to ride anything in the world, though one could feel the thin ribs and planking bend to the heave of water under one's knees.

We worked and traveled a lot also in the *Wavey*, an open twenty-foot boat with a single-cylinder four-horse inboard. The *Wavey* was a strong little boat, very good and very dry in a sea, and handy for beachcombing logs, as one could run her nose onto a good beach, if there was not too much swell. Ed had unlimited faith in her seagoing qualities and there were times when the sea seemed as close as it seemed in the canoe. We borrowed or traveled in or visited aboard many others of all shapes and sizes, seine boats and gill-net boats and fish-packers, camp boats, mission boats, trollers, even an occasional cruiser or yacht. And once we had a float-house, a shack on a raft of logs that we towed around to our logging so that we would have some place to live beside the boat.

The boat that did most work for us, and the finest sea boat of her size I have ever known, was Buster's troller, *Kathleen*. *Kathleen*, big by our standards, was thirty-two feet, with cabin and pilothouse, two after hatches and fourteen heavy horsepower. Buster took her anywhere, in any weather, and we were often intimate with the sea when the green swells battered themselves against the pilothouse windows. One night we ran her bow onto a shelving shingle beach in a storm and I went overboard with a heavy pry to hold her straight until the engine dragged her off. I grabbed for the bow as she slid away, thinking to pull myself aboard; but my thigh boots were full of water and I hadn't the strength, so I clung there, hollering for Buster and wondering whether to cut loose and try to swim back to shore. Buster supposed I had stayed ashore when the boat came away and heard nothing over the sound of the storm and the motor; but some seaman's sense brought him forward when *Kathleen* was clear and he found me there and pulled me aboard. I still wonder sometimes, in fact I'm wondering now, if I could have made the swim in thigh boots and a heavy Mackinaw.

We were in trouble at other times with *Kathleen*. Once a plug came loose in one of the live boxes when we had five tons of freight aboard. We tried to swing her towards shore, but a steering chain broke and there was nothing to do but leave the freight out on deck and bail until we could find the plug and drive it back. And once Buster took a big wave over the stern off Cape Mudge; it smashed in the pilothouse door and killed the engine and left him bailing for six long hours until the tide turned and the sea quieted and he could get started again. But I remember her best when we were working with her, towing a boom of logs through the calm night and into the next dawn, searching along a beach for stranded logs, swinging in to drop anchor and go ashore with the tools in the dinghy.

Buster was very proud of *Kathleen's* dinghy. It was eight feet long, clincher built, weighing forty-five pounds—an easy single-handed heave brought it clear up on deck or slid it over-side. But it was a tough little boat to launch from the beach in a swell; I tried three times one day and each time a wave caught it, pitched it back like a piece of cork, and left me sitting in water up to my neck. The next time we made it, but left the tools ashore for a calmer day. I saw *Kathleen* many times from water level, because Buster used to urge me to ride the logs out to the boat when he towed them off. We would jack one up into a good position, Buster would run in with *Kathleen* and throw me a tow line. Then I would drive a dog and set three or four turns of the line around the log; Buster would take a run with *Kathleen*, the log would roll and splash into the water, still rolling, and I would jump wildly for it. Sometimes it all went well; I stayed on and Buster slowed *Kathleen* and took in the towline, I stepped aboard, and we were ready to go again. Far too often for my self-respect I pitched into the water and had to steady the log and climb onto it again somehow, while Buster anxiously circled *Kathleen* to the rescue.

Now I travel more or less sedately in the police boat from time to time, to try a case somewhere out among the islands.

Or we charter sometimes cruisers, sometimes fishing boats, to go out and hunt ducks and geese and brant. I am still happy with it and the many pleasures and concerns of the sea come back at once, as though I had never been away from them.

I had not meant to write so much of boats or of the sea itself. My concern is rather with the edges of the sea, the beaches and bluffs and tideflats, the river mouths and the salt-water meadows. The British Columbia coast is rocky and mountainous; miles upon miles of its length are deep inlets and sounds, always with mountains rising steeply from the water to four or five thousand feet, and a boat can pass safely almost anywhere within a cable's length of the shore. But at the heads of the inlets and bays, where the rivers come down, there are meadows and sloughs and tideflats. This is the country of ducks and geese and bears and salmon. It is beyond the reach of roads, and I love it.

There are well-known places at the head of one or two of the longer inlets, where hunters go every year in some numbers. Usually we stay away from these and hunt out new places, guessing at their virtue from maps and charts, from rumor, and more rarely, dependable hearsay. There are many places. A lifetime would not hunt them all, a dozen lifetimes could not learn a tenth of them thoroughly. Yet each is one's own place for the time one is there; rocks and sandbars and tide changes become familiar; the twisting river channels, the potholes and sloughs of the meadows are learned and understood in a day or two; even the flight lines and the feeding patterns of the birds begin to take on some measure of predictability and shape. And there is always something new for the next day, another fork of the river, a chain of lakes inland beyond the meadow, another bay within the bay where the geese lighted or the ducks rafted during the shooting.

I can think of one deep bay we go to, wide open to the

northwesterlies, only a little better protected from the southeasters, where the widgeon feed by thousands. A little river comes in at the head of the bay and sandflats dotted with great rocks dry out from it for half a mile at low tide. Usually there are four of us hunting together and we go in very quietly, not shooting at all, two in the dinghy and two in the canoe. As we come near the head of the bay the widgeon begin to move, a few small flocks swing out past us, and the masses of birds feeding along the semicircular shoreline stir restlessly. Other flocks fly in or out, then one of the big concentrations, two or three thousand birds, takes wing in formidable sound. For a moment they are all together, white wing patches flashing, then they are a hundred smaller flocks swinging out, past us and over us. Other masses stir and go out until the beach is empty and something between five and ten thousand birds have left the stranded sea grasses at the tide's edge.

Long before we can reach the head of the bay and set out decoys, flocks of seven and ten and twenty or more birds are coming in again, sometimes circling and going out again, sometimes pitching and going back to their feeding as though they had never been disturbed, sometimes rising almost as they pitch.

We set out our few decoys, rarely more than half a dozen to each of us, hide ourselves, and wait. At first we shoot seriously, picking the baldpate widgeon drakes, watching carefully for the occasional mallard or pintail or shoveler. But the flocks come in and in on their swift wing beats, riding up the left side of the bay, swinging across the front of us, flickering towards the decoys, flaring away, turning back to the next set, often pitching a little way out or in between the sets. It no longer seems important to shoot, only to see and see and see, to watch the lovely flight, the swift turns and changes and twists, the setting of wings, the sudden drop and hissing pitch to the decoys. It is important to see the white-crowned head of the drake in flight, to catch the shine of green along its side, to feel the richness of the warm red-brown of breast and flank. The whole bay is movement and color and light, in mood and values that are never twice the same because weather changes everything. We have shot the bay in the face of a heavy northwester that drove alternations of ice-cold rain and pale sunshine across it on a rising tide; that was a day when the widgeon flew and flew with a wild determination lovely to watch. We have shot the long foreshore at dawn on a dead low tide and in evenings when the rocks stood black against pale water and pale sand; there have been calm days when the flocks came in more cautiously and with longer circlings and hesitations, but they still came; and windy days when great tides crowded us back into the salal brush along the edge of the timber, and the ducks swung to decoys set in the lee of a fallen spruce whose trunk and broken limbs were shaggy with seaweed from the swells sweeping over them.

When the first freshness of the thing is over, I usually take the canoe up the river channel, across the flats, through the narrow gap in the timber that is the river's real mouth, and into the first big circular pool. Teal and buffleheads and occasional mergansers start from the water ahead of the canoe, circle once, and pelt back past me. In the pool there are always mallards and more teal. They rise boldly, thirty or forty birds making a great stir in the enclosed place. The teal drive out, low and fast through the gap; most of the mallards climb swiftly and head up along the line of the river towards the lakes, but a few always turn back towards the guns outside.

Later, when the tide has built the pool back into the grasses at its edge, scattered groups of mallard come down from the lakes, high and fast along the river, cutting down suddenly towards the pool, flaring and twisting away with the built-up

speed still on them if we move to shoot. They are very difficult. But the last flight of the day is most difficult of all, so
spectacularly difficult that we always hold off and wait for it
and we rarely take more than two or three birds from it. It
comes just at dark, as we stand with our backs towards the tall
trees that close the pool off from salt water, our eyes straining
into the blue-grey of the sky upriver. Three hundred, five
hundred, perhaps a thousand or more mallard, for many are
beyond sight in the darkness, stream down from the lakes in
twenties and thirties and fifties, flock after flock, very high,
very fast. The whole problem is to see them soon enough,
flickers of deeper darkness against darkness. In the moment of
sight the gun must find shoulder and mark, then swing ahead
faster than the mind can believe it should to loose the charge
just short of the trees. Nearly always one is too late, often too
late to fire at all. But once in half a dozen times sight may be
quick enough, anticipation perfect, and a single bird will
crumple and crash into the trees on the seaward side of the
belt.

I have been told that geese use the bay sometimes, but have
never seen them there or found sign of them. Yet geese are our
true concern on these yearly hunts and any visit to the teem-
ing bay is only incidental to this main search. The great
western Canadas winter over in the lakes and salt-water
meadows of nearly every coast valley in British Columbia,
and the excitement of hunting them under these special conditions of wild and empty country, brown meadows, abrupt
mountains, hidden lakes, and strong rivers, is as keen as anything I know. It is not easy hunting, nor especially productive;
there is too much water and too much country for any casual
party of three or four hunters to be sure of results. But the
geese are always there and one plays for the breaks and
chances—a skillful stalk, a lucky choice of position, or a

moment of carelessness on the part of birds normally very cautious.

There is one estuary, a full mile width of flat clear meadows cut by a hundred deep sloughs, where the geese nearly always fly a line along the edge of the timber on a certain wind; that is as close as they come to predictability. There is another estuary of about the same width where a dozen shooters spread across the flats cannot be sure of anticipating their flight on any day that I have seen. There is a lagoon where they should come back through a narrow high-walled gut to open water— but often do not. There is a lake where they sometimes pitch in like mallards to a cluster of islands at the swampy end. There is a little narrow sound with high mountains at the head and along either side, and a sandspit stretching two-thirds of the way across it; it is an easy approach and should be a certain shot when geese are trapped in there. Yet I once saw a flock of fifty or sixty geese make a tight circle between the mountains and pass out over the sandbar so high that a rifle would hardly have reached them; I like to think that they found some freak updraft that lifted them, because that place also should be predictable.

Lately we have hunted a short inlet where two creeks enter side by side at the head. The right-hand creek swings sharply southward to a high pass that leads through to the head of another small inlet. It is a swift stream, full of salmon and with bears everywhere along its banks; we have found no place in its valley where geese would light. The other creek runs back a little way and turns through a right angle straight northward; its valley floor, between mountains as high as those of the other creek, is flat and wide. There is a big tidal meadow just beyond the right-angle turn and three lakes in less than three miles carry the valley almost through to a bay near the head of another long inlet. It is the perfect passageway for geese, and geese are always there, passing, resting, or feeding. We find them feeding in the meadows at dawn, find them again in the lakes, often see them passing high above the meadow through the day. Sometimes we get a shot at them; more often we do not.

It is hard to explain the fascination of Canada geese. I do not hunt primarily to kill them, but to be concerned with them. I am relieved rather than disappointed when the flock rises just beyond range, swings wide, or passes high; I love their name, their long black necks, the clean white cheek patches, the strong and heavy bodies. They mean courage to me, devotion, wisdom, endurance, and beauty, and I care not at all that the first three of these attributes should not normally be applied to creatures less than man. I go out to see them standing among tall grasses when they have not seen me, to find them floating serenely well out on still water and see them rise easily and powerfully from it. The measured slowness of the wing beat, the varying processional of ordered flight, the stretched necks, heads turning and watching, the voices talking, so plainly talking among themselves, all these things are strange and beautiful, with dignity and worth of their own. In cold reason, it seems fantastic to consider their destruction by gunshot; yet every emotion I feel from them is strengthened and deepened, at the moment and in recollection, by carrying a gun.

Later in the year we hunt another and smaller goose, the black sea brant. Brant are black and white birds and one hunts them in a black and white world. There are white snow and wet black rocks, white water, white snow flurries, black timber, white snow again on the open slopes of the mountains; grey sky, grey sand, grey beaches. The decoys, bobbing in strings and clusters in front of the blind, are black and white and the black heads of seals show often among them, stretching high out of the water to stare inquiringly at the blind, drawing calmly down without a sign of disturbed water, to show again still closer. White spouts and tall black fins of killer whales are often there and always black scoters, black cormorants, and black and white grebes. Sharpest black and white of all, seen against the pale water, are the little harlequin drakes that come in to ride with the decoys; white lines and dots of head and neck and breast and wing stand out plainly. Yet the harlequin is not black but mainly blue-grey, with a handsome patch of glowing ruby on either flank; this shows brilliantly through glasses and is visible sometimes even in the black and whiteness if one looks for it.

I like to shoot brant early, in December and January, before the migrating birds start to come through from the south. It is often a slow sport then, but the wintering brant are fat, fine birds and it seems a better triumph to understand and solve the problems they offer than to take advantage of the greenness of migrants. The brant is a true sea goose, markedly unwilling to cross anything drier than a tideflat or perhaps occasionally a sandspit. They ride out open-water storms in rafted comfort and come near shore only to feed on eelgrass or to find sand or gravel.

Brant shooting is mostly waiting and watching, broken by more active spells of moving the decoys and the blind as the tide rises and falls. It is usually cold, and often wet, but in spite of this one watches well and sees everything, for brant may come at any time and they can come in swiftly from a great distance. And the true reward is in watching. One sees first a wisp of black moving low over the water in the far distance—perhaps cormorants, perhaps scoters, perhaps brant. Then it is a line of dark birds in swift, even flight, not scoters because it rises or falls in flight, swings out and comes back to line; not cormorants because the rise and fall of flight is even, from level to level, where cormorants jerk upwards singly, bird by bird. They come on and on, twenty or thirty feet above the water, very swiftly, very gracefully; and suddenly are passing the decoys or swinging into them.

When birds have passed or come in and been fired on, one waits again. Gulls hunt clams, fly up and drop them on rocks to break them open; crows shadow the gulls and wait their chance of theft or leavings. Eagles search over the water, ravens pass smoothly about their business, a hawk or a flicker shows on the landward side. In the water between one's feet are mussels, little crabs, barnacles, and sea anemones of many colors, purple or brown, translucent green or grey. A red-breasted merganser drops to the decoys and swims in puzzled friendliness up and down the bobbing line. A flight of black birds far out seems for a moment like brant, but the glasses show cormorants. A flock of Aleutian sandpipers pitches briefly on the beach in front of the blind, then rises and flickers away to pitch again two or three hundred feet farther along.

Last season we found a new sand beach and hunted it for brant. The weather was bad and they came sparsely, in twos and threes for the most part, often passing wide of us and carrying on to some more favored place. I began to think the beach was not as good as it seemed. The last evening we worked it was the day after a savage snowstorm with a fifty-mile easterly gale. It was a cold evening with a northeast breeze and heavy snow clouds piled in enormous density over the Vancouver Island mountains. The sun went redly down behind them, somehow forcing its color through the mass. I watched a long reach of wave-rippled sand and tried to keep close enough to the edge of the tide as it drew swiftly away over the level beach. Then the brant came, a great flock of two hundred or more, black, slow-winged, and confident against the piled red clouds over the Golden Hind. They swung for the decoys, swung away, some of them calling, circled once, then pitched on the rippled water fifty yards outside my decoys. They packed immediately, as brant so often do, until there seemed no space between any two of them. But they were suspicious. Long necks raised uneasily. The flock let itself drift on the wind, a little towards shore but away from me at the same time, down towards the center of the sandy bay. I left the blind and began to stalk them over open sand, but they knew and drifted faster. There seemed no hope unless I could somehow herd them down towards Buckie and George on the point at the other side of the bay.

So I stood up and began to wade straight out until the wavelets splashed over my boot tops, then I turned towards the brant again. There was hope now. I was almost outside them, and upwind of them, with the dark of eastern sky and water behind me. Slowly I waded, herding them steadily downwind, towards the point half a mile away. They kept their distance, eighty or a hundred yards from me, watching me curiously, talking among themselves, riding the little swells with the lovely buoyancy that brant seem to have above all water birds. I saw Buckie move on the point and go back to cover. A hundred yards more, I thought, and someone must have a chance. The hundred yards became fifty. They had to rise into the wind, which would bring them past me unless they swung at once. And if they did that they would be within reach of the point. Twenty-five yards more. There was no change in the flock. They were still drifting at the same speed, still a little anxious, still talking among themselves. Then suddenly, all together, they rose, dead into the wind, wide of me, wide of the point. Jet black birds against the pale sky and water, a few voices kronking protest, slow wings;

then they turned out a little into the cold red sky and were gone.

It was a brant hunter's unorthodoxy, fifteen or twenty minutes of utter fascination, more memorable than any triumph that yielded dead birds.

LET THEM EAT SAWDUST

I HAVE BEEN, ALL MY LIFE, WHAT is known as a conservationist. I am not at all sure that this has done myself or anyone else any good, but I am quite sure that no intelligent man, least of all a countryman, has any alternative. It seems clear beyond possibility of argument that any given generation of men can have only a lease, not ownership, of the earth; and one essential term of the lease is that the earth be handed on to the next generation with unimpaired potentialities. This is the conservationist's concern.

It is in the history of civilizations that conservationists are always defeated, boomers always win, and the civilizations always die. I think there has never been, in any state, a conservationist government, because there has never yet been a people with sufficient humility to take conservation seriously. This is natural enough. No man is intimately concerned with more than his lifetime, comparatively few men concern themselves seriously with more than a fraction of that time; in the last analysis all governments reflect the concerns of the people they govern, and most modern democratic governments are more deeply concerned with some brief, set term of office than with anything else. Conservation means fair and honest dealing with the future, usually at some cost to the immediate present. It is a simple morality, with little to offset the glamor and quick material rewards of the North American deity, "Progress."

Living near a settlement like Elkhorn one sees both sides of the argument lived out, and inevitably takes part. Elkhorn is entirely dependent on natural resources in their first state. Almost the whole of Vancouver Island is, or was, timber; possibly the finest softwood saw-log timber in the world. Next in importance to timber are the recreational assets—game, game fish, and scenery; after these, commercial fishing, coal mining, agriculture, and water power. Elkhorn is touched by all of them, but timber is overwhelmingly the most important factor in its existence; the whole forty-year life of the village has been built on service to the logging camps and loggers of the surrounding country. And during those years the importance of a tourist trade based mainly on sport fishing has steadily increased.

It would be logical to suppose that everyone in Elkhorn would be interested in forestry and forest conservation, but almost no one is. Vancouver Island's forests were at first considered "inexhaustible"; then, as it became clear that they were being rapidly exhausted, the forests became an expendable asset, to be used in "opening up the country" so that some unspecified phenomenon, probably "industry," could come in and take over. In spite of some very halfhearted attempts at a sounder forest policy by the government, that is where things rest at present. Elkhorn and other little towns like it watch the big logging camps draw farther and farther away as the more accessible timber is cleared off; they know vaguely that the end of saw-log timber is in sight, that millions of deforested acres are reproducing only slowly if at all; yet they retain a mystic faith in the future, a belief that "progress" in the shape of roads and wharves and airplanes and hydroelectric power will somehow lead them on to a continuously more abundant life. Perhaps they will. But even that could not excuse or justify the fire-destroyed acres, the incredible waste of timber in logging, the long barren years through which magnificent forest land has grown little or nothing.

Elkhorn is in no way unique. This frantic dream of progress and development has cursed nearly every hamlet and village in North America at some time or another, bringing with it premature sidewalks and false-front stores, fantastic real-estate projects, fierce neon signs and an orgy of public services planned with a solidity that might better have gone into the jerry-built houses. Usually it is a recurrent frenzy, starting with each sizable economic boom, dying back between whiles to surge up again on some new promise of oil or minerals or large construction, any high and easy road to sudden wealth. And it is not wholly bad. It has built a continent's material civilization, blatantly, wastefully, with an enormous cruelty in the shattering of men's hopes and dreams, and frequent distortions of true values; but it has built it, and perhaps it was necessary to build so fast and so extravagantly.

But now that the continent is crossed and secured the method seems stupid, the haste merely destructive. The sanctity of "progress" with its tricky little catch phrase, "We can't stand in the way of progress," seems suddenly false and treacherous. It is a good time to ask, "Why can't we?", to pull progress apart and take a new look at it, to examine everything called "development" in terms of values that already exist, in its relationship to the economy of the whole nation and the whole continent; above all, in its relationship to human happiness.

Progress seems to mean, all too often, the projection of slums into the wilderness. Incredibly, for all its village size, Elkhorn achieved slums for itself on land that had been bush only a year previously. This came about in a sudden flux of temporary jobs on a major construction project; people poured in, found high wages, then paid higher rents for tar-paper shacks set in mud, where each family shared a single room and a dozen families shared a hand pump for water, and an outside toilet. The project was finished, many of the families moved out and the village had time to wonder what had happened to it. Meanwhile the timber has drawn back two or three years farther into the mountains. But more people than ever before are dependent on it.

So the more abundant life has arrived briefly and departed, much of it spent in failure and waste. High wages have little meaning if they will buy only tar-paper shacks as transient homes for growing children. Boom and progress and development add up to high real-estate prices, houses scattered among vacant lots that no one can afford to buy, a few short lengths of sidewalk, some no-parking signs, and a multiplicity of stores with little reason to be doing business. And the village settles back to consolidate. Strangely, there is something to consolidate. More people are living in the community, even though there is apparently less reason for them to be doing so. There is a framework of community organization, something beyond the simple mutual help of the older days. There are many improved services, such strange exotic things as street lights and an up-to-date water system and an extremely modern school. Some of these things may prove difficult to maintain and pay for; but they exist and merely by doing so they make a village out of what had been only a settlement. Somehow timber and tourists will support them until another boom comes and a few more of the vacant lots between the houses are filled and a small town begins to grow out of the village. But the solidity, the real existence of the town, as of the village, will be built only slowly, between the booms.

It is difficult to know how much or how little human happiness grows out of such a boom, but the total seems less than before. There are more worried and anxious and uncertain people than there were before. Even small businessmen who have done well are strained by their expansion, working harder, worrying more, remembering the quieter, more logical times with regret. Even the most ambitious of them speak regretfully of simplicities they loved in the earlier Elkhorn, which now seem lost in the surge of progress they called for. Yet they must seem to call for more progress because the deity is sacrosanct; no North American businessman can deny her lip service, no matter what may be in his heart.

A conservationist fights many battles, varying in scale all the way from the attempted protection of some individual species of wildlife to the supreme issue of proper use of soil, air, and water; and every fight is complicated, if not forced, by the false urgency and outdated sanctity of progress. The speed of modern development is such that the conservationist is always under attack, rarely has time himself to attack. He needs only breathing space, a little time for thought to creep in and temper progress with wisdom. Development is rarely a matter of urgency. Timber, soil, fisheries, oil and minerals, even water power, become more, not less, valuable with delay. The problem is to use the self-reproducing resources within their safe yield and to develop the wasting resources without injury to others already producing.

Elkhorn, when a government was damming its river, had to fight and fight hard to save the salmon run on which its tourist trade is built. She had to fight again, still harder, to win clearing of the land that would be flooded by the dam. She expects, and needs, a pulp mill; probably it will come one day and if it does she will have to fight again, harder than ever before, to save her waters from pollution.

Such conflicts as these go on throughout the continent, and none of them is necessary. Hydroelectric developments, pulp mills, and other such manifestations of progress are not dreamed up overnight. There is always ample time for mature and careful consideration of every issue involved. But early planning is always left to the single-track minds of the developers, often buried in deepest secrecy for purely commercial reasons, and the conservationist is left with a last-ditch battle. In this way the burden of proof is always forced upon him. He is standing in the way of progress—reactionary, narrow, without real vision.

It seems clear to me that all destruction it causes should be reckoned in the direct cost of any project, and that no preventable destruction should ever be permitted. Obviously flooded land is no longer land in any useful sense; but it should be cleared of timber and debris before flooding so that a lake with good bottom and clean shores will take its place. If the cost of this is too great for the project to bear, then the project is uneconomic. Runs of game and commercial fish can be destroyed by poorly planned dams; but sound planning can always find some way to compensate and may even save the whole resource. The onus here is just as clear, if not clearer, since a run of fish properly looked after will maintain itself indefinitely into the future, while a hydroelectric development may be outdated within twenty years, almost certainly will be within fifty years. Pollution of air and water by industrial plants is the simplest issue of all. There are adequate means of preventing all such pollutions. Admittedly they are sometimes costly, but if the industry cannot support the cost it is economically unsound. No nation can afford polluted air or polluted waterways.

These are sweeping statements, and I mean them to be. A civilization built on foul air and polluted water, on destroyed timber lands, overgrazed ranges, exhausted farm lands, on water sucked from one river system to make cheap electricity on another, is too costly and too insecurely based to last. I saw recently a newspaper editorial happily forecasting that before very long the world's timber supplies will be too valuable for any such simple use as building houses or making paper; they will all be needed for human food—processed, no doubt, into pulpy palatability, but still essentially sawdust. Any civilization that can cheerfully contemplate such a morbid future for its multiplied grandchildren needs a new philosophy.

Industrial development has produced such an enormous material prosperity, so widely spread, that its sanctity is easy to understand. But in North America it has done so largely by using capital assets as income. That is why conservation is now far more important than further development. It seems to me that the people of the continent, both Canadians and Americans, have everything to gain, nothing to lose, by stopping to take stock and understand what they have got and how it can soundly be used. Exhausting a continent and overpopulating it to the point at which its inhabitants must start eating trees seems a strange way to a more abundant life.

It is difficult to believe the theorists who say that a nation to be sound must have an increasing population. Thousands of years ago the human race had to breed tolerably fast to survive. After that nations had to grow large populations in fear of wars. And there was always the idea that man must multiply until he had overrun the earth. He seems to have achieved this and surely he can be allowed to pause to recognize that there is no virtue in population for the sake of population; if there were, India, China, even Russia would be more prosperous nations than they are. It is difficult to believe that there is any true morality in producing children, or any essential immorality in not producing them. Certainly there is little to be said for raising men to be slaves to "progress" and cities, to industry and all the machines of a civilization frantically producing substitutes for the natural things it has destroyed.

Conservation is wise use of natural resources, which ultimately are the whole life of any country, even one that imports most of its natural resources. And it is axiomatic that no special interest, whether it is industrial or governmental, can be trusted to use raw materials wisely. All resources are interdependent; soil, for instance, cannot be separated from water tables, nor water tables from forests; and all life that moves on the land, in the water, or in the air is affected by every use of these resources. Government departments work independently and with blind irresponsibility to achieve specialized departmental ends; British Columbia has an Electric Power Act that restricts the function of a powerful commission to the production of cheap electricity; it has a Water Act that recognizes fourteen uses for water, but does not include its use by fish, though the commercial salmon fishery is one of the three or four main resources of the province. The logging industry has to pay only slight attention to forest regeneration, none at all to economical use of timber stands, preservation of soil or water resources. So it is through the whole picture. The conservationist's hope—perhaps dream is the better word—is to change all this, to establish a coordination of effort that will make sure that every factor is properly weighed and every resource fully protected against exploitation or wanton destruction. There are a few slow signs that we are beginning to think on these lines; the existence of a minor government department called the Land Utilization Branch is one of them, and an annual conference of experts on natural resources initiated by this branch is another. But this is a feeble result for the last west, with a whole continent's lessons of waste and destruction to draw on. Perhaps I take too much pleasure in prophesying doom, perhaps I am too much countryman and woodsman to understand the dream of progress through cities and machines, to feel the romance of the bulldozer and the earth mover, the concrete mixer and the four-lane highway. But I think we are on our way through the whole tragic story, that we shall live well on it. Our children and grandchildren and great-grandchildren will have to solve the slow, difficult problem of restoration as best they can. Perhaps atomic power will help them. It seems to be our only legacy.

JANUARY

Snow in a normally wet climate can be formidably persistent. A winter's snow in our coast mountains will pile to a depth of twenty-five or thirty feet or more; we expect that and in large measure live on it; it makes the character of the mountains, ensures the steady summer flow of streams and rivers, fills lakes, maintains water tables, draws the salmon runs and gives them their chance of increase. Down here at sea level there will be a little snow at Christmastime and more, perhaps a couple of feet, in January. But every so often pressures build differently, air masses move in different patterns, and the snow persists in fall after fall until there are several feet on the ground, even at sea level. It becomes formidable then, massive and confining, a threat to many things.

We have had this year a succession of minor snowfalls—ten inches, a foot, perhaps eighteen inches at a time. The first fall was heavy and wet. It clung to trees and broke them, tore down telephone lines and power lines, bowed the limbs of evergreens until forest trees had the conical shape of ornamentals. The cold followed immediately, then more snow. Roofs and buildings collapsed down in the village, the sheep huddled under the conifers in one corner of the pasture, Primrose stirred from the barn only occasionally and reluctantly; we shoveled roofs and paths and driveways and supposed there would be a thaw. But we have no right to expect a thaw in January and there has been none, only more and more snow. Shoveling snow has become a daily routine of survival.

There are many compensations. One has to be out and doing; true, the urgencies of ordinary living are still there and just as urgent, the letters to be answered, the book to be written, the lawyers to be listened to; but it is still more urgent to save the chicken-house roof after the first cracks have shown in the sheeting, to get water to the cow, hay and oats to the sheep, to clear the mailbox and cut a path for the feed man to bring in his sacks. The few people one sees are friendly and helpful. The great bulldozers that thunder down from the camps with snow flowing away from their thirteen-foot angle blades are enormously impressive in the little road. The dead leaves on the oak tree in the driveway have many sounds; a dry rustle in the north wind, a fainter whisper under falling snowflakes, sounds like little drums when the snow is harder and wind-driven.

The little birds are round the house as usual in snow; juncos, towhees, song sparrows, magnificent orange-shafted flickers, handsome dark blue jays. The swamp robins have not come this year for some reason, and the chickadees hold back, seemingly able to find what they need in the woods. Apart from the jays, the juncos and towhees are most persistent and dependent; sometimes I threaten to shoot some of the jays, but I never do because they have lived side by side with the others through many winters and all have survived. For the same reason I spare the occasional sharp-shinned hawk that sweeps in to take its toll. Perhaps there will be a junco or a towhee the less for his coming, but that's his affair and theirs, not mine. The eternally flickering white tail feathers of the juncos and their quick movement to the protection of brush or trees are their survival.

The great dark birds, eagles and crows and ravens, move anxiously overhead all day. The crows are sometimes searching, sometimes clustered at a find. The ravens seem bewildered but determined, crossing and recrossing the pastures on slow wings, sometimes perching briefly to speak a musical protest from a treetop. The eagles fly almost violently up and down the river, screaming often, sweeping up to perch magnificently in the leaning spruce on the far bank, scattering powdery snow from the weighted branches as they do so. Nearly every morning one or two are high in the big fir, whistling to others, usually juveniles, in flight. They rarely seem to feed when I am watching them and I have found no purpose in their movements.

On New Year's Day there was a heavy snowfall on a strong north wind, and I knew it was time to clear snow from the big flat-roofed dormers we have added to the house. With shovel or scraper it is weary work because nothing will slide, every cubic foot of snow must be lifted and moved or pushed to its descent. I felt hardly used, by the weather, by the enormous roof space of my house, by the consistency of the snow and the inadequacy of my shovel. Then I heard the bugle voices, faintly at first on the wind but coming closer. I looked towards the sound and hoped and they came, low, straight over the house, necks stretched, great wings in slow and powerful beat, three trumpeter swans. They were less white than the falling snowflakes and almost lost among them, for all their size and nearness, but I could see the jet black legs held tight against their heavy bodies, clear-cut lines like feathers, and even the blackness of the beaks, the shadow of the eyes. They were gone too quickly, across the river and out of sight beyond the ridge on the far side. But I no longer felt even faintly sorry for myself.

Happily, too, in this time the schools have been closed and the children home. No child of mine, left to itself, is a willing worker. But they can be talked into it if there is time enough to talk, and so long as the old man is around to goad and reproach and argue they can achieve surprising things. We cleared the garage and cottage roofs for the second, or maybe the third time in the late afternoon of a clear cold day. I put on snowshoes and used the big scraper from below, dragging down snow in satisfying avalanches. They were all over the roof, two-year-old Celie with them, the black Labrador running excitedly along the ridge pole. For five or ten minutes at a stretch we would be solemnly industrious. Alan would decide to slide. A sister, outraged by such idleness, would assist the slide. Alan would finish up deep in a snowbank and call on me to rescue him. Celie, somehow released from the roof, came tottering round the cleared place in front of the garage, ventured into my snowshoe track, and found it too much for her. I cut her a snow seat, upholstered it with a Mackinaw, and she was warm and happy.

From the roof Alan said, "The big stump makes a snow picture. You ought to take it for a Christmas card, Daddy. All white except for one black spot."

"Don't listen to him, Daddy," Mary said. "He's trying to get out of working."

"No," I said. "A true child of British Columbia. A blackened stump is part of life." I meant it too and tried to see it with his eyes, the blackened stump, familiar to him through his life, in all his play over by the barn, in all his waiting for school busses, made suddenly white and unfamiliar.

"You always stick up for him, just because he's a boy," Valerie said. And Alan came off the roof into the snowbank again. Mary chose the moment to slide down, staggered Valerie in passing. Valerie tottered a moment, then slid too. I untangled the pile, expecting tears and found only laughter.

As we finished the roof the sun was set and the children noticed its reflected color in the surface of the snow. They noticed the blue light where the reflection did not strike, noticed the wind ripples on the fields and compared them to the wave ripples on sand as the tide goes down. Maybe they shouldn't have to work.

This year's snow and cold are not over yet. It is still below zero outside. It is hard now to find a place to put the snow we clear from the lower roofs. I don't know how much has fallen, probably a total of six or eight feet that has packed to something less than five feet. Unless a chinook comes soon it will be the deepest snow and the longest winter we have ever had. Yet the falls have been so intermittent, so individually gentle, and with so little wind that none of them is memorable. Fifteen years ago, on our first wedding anniversary, there was a memorable snow. A dry blizzard drove on an easterly gale through a day and a night to pile five feet of new snow on eighteen inches of old. We knew we couldn't expect the roads to be opened again for two or three weeks and cared not at all.

The day after the storm there were roofs to be shoveled. I was working near the gate when a group of six men came along the road on snowshoes. My friend Herbert was in the lead and I asked him where they were going. "There's a party of big shots marooned up at the lake," he said. "We've got to break a trail through for them to come out on."

"Want me to come along?" I asked.

"No," he said. "I guess there's enough of us." He glanced at the roof I had been working on. "You've got plenty of your own to do."

So I cleared my roofs and cut my paths and towards dark went into the house. Herbert came as we were starting supper.

"We didn't do so well," he said. "Only two of us had been on snowshoes before and we had to turn back at the fork."

Less than three miles out of seven, I thought. Herbert was a fine woodsman and a good walker. "You could have made it," I said.

"I guess I could, but the others couldn't. The idea was to break enough trail for them to come out on easily."

"Want me to try it?"

"Would you? I can line up two men to go with you."

We started shortly after six, with light packs of food and other comforts for the big shots, and three flashlights. It was a black night, with new snow falling in heavy flakes, but the broken trail was easy to follow and I slipped swiftly and happily along it. I was down the first hill and at the creek crossing before I realized there was no one behind me. I waited a little, then turned back and found my helpers floundering at the top of the hill. Neither had worn snowshoes before.

"It's a long trip," I said. "You sure you want to go on?"

"There'll be five bucks in it," Roy Price said. "I'd go to hell and back for five bucks."

"That's right," Al said. "We need the money. You lead the way and we'll follow somehow."

I tightened their harnesses, did what little I could to tell them and show them how to stay upright, and we started out again. I came to the end of the broken trail at the fork, went on a few steps into the smooth snow and knew it was going to be a tough night. It was eight-fifteen exactly; one way or another we had been two hours covering three miles over broken trail. Herbert had said the party would be on its way out from the lake and we should meet them somewhere, but it seemed unlikely they would make more than a mile or two at the far end. Roy and Al came up at last. They were still cheerful, but they had fallen many times. "These things keep coming off," Roy said. "And when they don't come off they nose-dive." So we worked on his harness again. They still wanted to come.

"Look," I said. "It's going to be a long trip. I'm going to break right through to the falls turning and you come on in your own time. Turn back if you want, but don't go off my trail whatever you do."

I started out happily. My shoes plowed a foot or more into the powdery snow at each step, but it shook cleanly from them and I found I could make two or three hundred paces at a time without stopping. For a while the lights were in sight behind me, then I lost them. Suddenly I realized it was hard to follow the narrow road. Snow was drifted across it in great ridges and the gullies between the ridges looked far more like the road than the road itself. I cursed myself for not bringing a compass, yet felt I knew where I was going and at the same time mistrusted the feeling. The snow had almost stopped falling and it was a still night. In a little while I could hear the sound of the falls, a mile or so away to the north, and knew that my direction was right. Half an hour later I came to the signpost at the falls turning, almost buried in the snow but the first clear evidence I had had that the road was still underfoot. I went on, around the big bend and into the timber to look for lights on the long straight stretch ahead. There were none, so I turned back again to find my friends. I was suddenly worried that they might have missed my trail, or, far worse, stopped to open the bottled comfort they were carrying for the big shots. I found them, still half a mile short of the signpost, still cheerful and determined. I asked Roy about the bottles. "Don't worry," he said. "We won't touch it till you say. That bottled stuff's no good to travel on."

"Just so you say sometime before we get there," Al said. "They can have what's left."

I knew then we would make it and went on with a quiet mind. It was peaceful and quiet in the timber and a moon had come up behind the snow clouds to make the night almost light. The snow seemed heavier and cut me back to seventy-five or a hundred steps between rests, but I broke the mile length of the straight stretch and had come back over most of my track before I saw the lights rounding the curve.

"Time for the bottle yet?" Al asked.

"No," I said. "We've got all of two miles to go."

"They must of broke some trail from their end."

"I'll believe it when I see it," I said. "First snowshoe print I see I'll stop and we'll open a bottle right there."

I left them again, circled the first little lake, followed the slough almost to the curve below Jim's lodge on the big lake, then turned and came back. I found Al and Roy halfway along the little lake.

"This it?" Al asked.

"This is it," I said. "One here, all you want at the next stop."

We opened a bottle and each took a good pull at it. "Jeez," Roy said. "I'm going to sleep for a couple of days when we get there."

"Jim'll give you a bed," I told him. "You've earned it."

I went on to the lodge then. Jim seemed to be out of bed almost at the sound of my hand on the door. "Breakfast," he said. "We'll have it right away."

I looked at my watch, saw it was 4:00 A.M., and hoped my own reaction would have been as right. "I've got to collect my partners," I told Jim. "We'll be along quick as we can make it."

I met them just at the end of the slough and we squatted in the snow and punished the opened bottle thoroughly.

"Five bucks," Roy said. "If it wasn't for the times I've had to pull up my pants I'd say it was easy money." Roy's suspenders had broken on the first hill.

"I've seen easier," Al said. "But this here's something on the side." He tilted the bottle again, for a long half minute.

We had breakfast and Roy and Al went off to bed. But I wanted to get home before my legs stiffened, so I slipped out with the first daylight. Our trail was good, clear and clean and hard-packed, and my snowshoes sang their way along it. The trees were dark green, heavy and drooping with white, everything else was pure white shading into the pale grey sky; only two colors in the world, no sound, no movement in all of it except my own. The long straight stretch was nothing. The hill round the big bend to the buried signpost was a few sliding steps. The level stretch where the snow had drifted the road away was plain, friendly trail. I met Herbert on his way up to meet me at the far end of it. Less than an hour later we were home and as we passed through the gate we felt a warm breeze on our faces and a few drops of rain. The thaw had started.

ART OR SCIENCE

From time to time, in misguided moments, I used to say in public that I write books to make money. It always surprised me, and often annoyed me a little, to find that this upset most of the people who heard me. I used to wonder why they should consider it estimable in a banker to bank for money, in a manufacturer to manufacture, a policeman to police, a lawyer to argue, a farmer to plow, all for money, but quite outrageous for a writer to write for money. What better, I wondered, do they want of me than a professional job? And doesn't a writer have to eat, same as anyone else?

I felt very hard-boiled and realistic when I was thinking all that, very professional and competent. But it occurs to me now that what I said was quite wrong and that my hearers were quite right to be upset. I don't write books solely or even primarily to make money; if I did I should certainly write different books. Nor am I very deeply concerned about money; if I were I should turn to some sensible occupation, like manufacturing automobiles or digging ditches. What I do is write books and hope occasionally that they will make enough money for me to go on eating and writing books. And I think that is true of a satisfying number of people, including people who dig ditches and manufacture automobiles.

The fact remains, though, that in writing I am a professional and undoubtedly am influenced by so being. I fit my writing into fairly tidy, more or less traditional forms, choose subjects that I think will interest other people as well as myself, handle them within limits that I hope will pass censorships and other such tests. I do not know whether I write better or worse because my living depends on it; a surprising number of the world's great writers have not needed to write for a living. I do not know whether my pleasure in writing is greater or less because I am a professional. I do know that my conscience is clearer about the time I spend in writing than it would be otherwise, and I know that my effort is greater, more disciplined, more thorough.

January

In all things except writing I am an amateur by choice and in the original sense of the word; I do the things I do for the love of doing them. In a world full of experts, and intensive and high specialization, the word has developed a vaguely derogatory meaning—it began to do so at least as far back as the start of the nineteenth century—but I concede no shade of this. I believe that amateurism is the world's lost youth and hope and delight; I believe it is the finest and potentially the most productive devotion that can be given.

What I mean is most easily demonstrated in sport. There is not a sport in the world that has not grown out of amateurism, away from people doing the thing for the love of it. So far as I know that's the only logic there is in sport. But in most sports today the amateur is merely someone who doesn't take money quite so openly as a professional. I suppose American college football is the outstanding example. Presumably the original idea of it was to give the students a little fun and a little exercise; then the schools started making money out of it, began to pay out money to make more money, complicated the game to a spectator's orgy, and killed the sport. Students don't play football any more; they can't compete with professionals and the game is not meant to be fun anyway, except to watch. So they get their exercise sitting in the stands and watching. The remarkable thing is that they don't complain. I'm always hopeful that some revolutionary campus committee will one day start a movement to give the game back to the kids.

The same is true of most other sports that can be turned into box-office spectacles. The amateur boxer is just a young fellow not quite ready to turn professional; the amateur hockey player doesn't make quite a whole-time job of it; professional baseball has such amazing precision and finish that little is heard of school or college teams and most boys who have attained the age of self-consciousness seem ashamed to play the game at all. All this adds up to a wonderful time for sports writers and promoters, but I think it is also the greatest loss of positive pleasure in the history of the world.

I began to play golf rather frequently when I was about sixteen and I always remember how indignant grandfather was. "Another sport," he said angrily. "You'll always be jack of all trades and master of none. Why don't you settle down to one and be good at it?"

He had a point, of course. I was playing three brands of football at the time, as well as rackets, handball, and cricket; I was running and jumping and boxing in schoolboy competition, swimming a little, sailing occasionally, managing to enjoy them all and find time to turn most of my energy to hunting and fishing. I have never mastered any sport, and two or three years later I had dropped them all except hunting and fishing. But it was a lot of fun while it lasted and not at all too hard to be worth a place on a team—of fellow amateurs.

At that time I had not the conviction about amateurism that I have now, only an instinct for it. Against that instinct, I seriously thought of becoming a professional in some competitive sport. And later I actually became a professional hunter and trapper and guide. I was young enough and sufficiently free from responsibility not to take my professionalism too seriously; but I was surprised to find how quickly keenness of pleasure dulled into routine. I dropped the professionalism and found my sharp pleasures again.

I wonder sometimes now about my simon-pure standing as a fisherman, a hunter, or a naturalist. I write about hunting and fishing and nature, and I believe that is reckoned enough in some sports to put one over the line. But I don't fish or hunt or watch in order to write; I do so to please myself, because I enjoy doing it; and I haven't a professional's expert qualifications in any of the three sports. So I claim amateur standing and I believe I need it; to know and write adequately of pleasures one must be an amateur. Which makes me, I suppose, a professional amateur, and brings the argument full cycle.

What I am trying to say is that specialization is hell; I use this last word in full reverence, with a respectful nod in the direction of all those stories that end with the Devil saying, "That's the hell of it." In narrowest logic it would seem that the more expert one becomes in anything, the greater the pleasure that can be derived from it. But a danger of expertness that comparatively few men seem able to avoid is an obsessive narrowness that stifles pleasure and may well stifle imagination. The amateur's true joy and true virtue is in his wide frame of reference, in the many points of feeling and understanding at which experience touches experience and broadens both to liven imagination. Of all living men, the freest and the richest may well be Winston Churchill. Even if one grants that he is a three-fold professional, as statesman and writer and orator, he is still an amateur of more interests than fill most men's lives; a brilliant and successful amateur of history and strategy, of painting and bricklaying, brandy and cigars; amateur soldier, farmer, seaman, horseman, perhaps of other arts and crafts as well. Since he is far more successful in his professions than the most devoted of single-track specialists, it is difficult not to suppose that all these amateurisms contribute to his ability as well as express it.

With the shade of grandfather glancing over my shoulder, I hesitate to admit the number and shallowness of my own amateurisms. Yet when I stop to remember him it is clear to me that the old gentleman was himself a manifold amateur. Lawyer by training, businessman by choice, he found time to be a skilled amateur of wine and Wellington, of horses, farms, pheasants, and the antiquities of his county. He even found time to publish a thick volume on the Old Stone Crosses of Dorset and a slender paper or two on such features of the county as dew ponds and avenues. And he acknowledged his professional training only to the extent of sitting in simon-pure amateurism as Justice of the Peace.

I think my own most intense amateurism is the Bench, and in spite of my boldest convictions I often suspect its value. There is a precision in legal thinking, a slowly developed codification of human probabilities that the lay mind cannot always follow as it should. At the same time, nearly all the more difficult cases one hears are largely a matter of deciding which of two quite plausible witnesses is lying on certain essential points; the probability that both sides are lying on some points does not simplify things at all, but it removes the problem even farther from solution by legal routine. Between decision and sentence, legal training is of little value; one is bound by certain legal limits that are often none too humane, but there is a plain duty to exercise the utmost humanity within those limits. When I try to imagine myself sitting with the security and confidence of a professional, I feel more secure as I am. As an amateur I have no excuses, I can be in no haste, I can consider nothing routine or easy. I must find my reward in the difficulties and complications of human nature or go without reward.

I have played, almost to the verge of professionalism, with ichthyology. My interest in fish grew out of the sport of catching them and for a while became far stronger than the sport itself. It led me into study of migration and feeding, flow and temperature of water, a thousand relationships between fish and other fish, fish and insects, crustaceans, beetles, weeds, even the chemical content of water. I worked over commercial catch records, commercial methods of using fish, commercial controls and harvests and escapements, and in time I became something that a layman might reasonably mistake for an expert. Then someone suggested that I take on the job of running an enormous game fishery, and I knew I had gone too far. I wanted to know fish well enough to write about them, to catch them, and to watch them with understanding and satisfaction. But I did not want to be a fish specialist, committed to fish for the rest of my life. So I relaxed a little, turned back to being an angler rather than an ichthyologist, and preserved my amateur standing. Now I can go fishing and watch fish again with a calm, receptive mind; I don't have to explore the insides of every fish I catch or read his scales under a microscope, I don't have to study the temperature and height of the water every time I go out, I don't have to prove everything I think about fish before I think it. I can if I want, but I don't have to. I have no regrets about the measure of expertness I did attain; it adds to the quality of every other interest I have and rounds the pleasure I now find in fishing to something approaching completeness; but I want to use it, not be used by it.

I should not suggest that there must be a limit to the expertness of the amateur. An amateur may be as expert or inexpert as he likes, so long as his mind remains free from specialization, so long as he is not limited to a scientific or legal or literary or some other specialized habit of thought, so long as he retains a capacity for wonder and speculation and delight, so long as he remains an ordinary rather than a specialized human. The amateur's essential quality is to love his subject without thought of material reward; his function, if he needs one, is to bridge the gap between specialization and ordinary humanity and, more rarely, to supply imagination where specialization has killed it.

When I fill out one of those questionnaires that are forced upon all men periodically throughout their lives, I usually list my "hobbies" as book-collecting and farming. Sometimes I add carpentering and watching baseball. This last is a shame that I cannot avoid. Of all games baseball is the one I should most like to have played, but I was introduced to it so late in life that I am fit to play only with my children, and shall not much longer be fit for that. But the beauties and intricacies of the game, its speed and constant tension fascinate me so completely that I cannot tear myself away from the most minor bush-league game without watching and hoping through the very last play. Yet I am not an amateur of baseball, for amateurism is nothing so negative as watching. In somewhat the same way, I doubt if I am a true amateur of farming or carpentering. I love to look at good farming, I get some satisfactions from my own minor attempts at it; but I doubt if anything less than a yield of butter and eggs and meat and milk would ever persuade me to put in a couple of hours a day as nursemaid and midwife to chickens and cows and sheep. My carpentry is done mostly in a state of absorbed frustration; I would always rather be doing something else and my concern is to make something, fast and fitted, to serve some purpose of Ann or the children or myself. My reward is a glow of righteous satisfaction when the job is done and not too badly done. But there is something less than amateur integrity in it.

"Book-collecting" sounds well on the questionnaires. There is a feeling of leisured wealth about it, of taste and erudition and discrimination; to none of which I can lay claim. Yet I am a true amateur. No Cotton or Parker or Roxburghe ever searched more diligently than I do, no Smith or Rosenbach ever felt greater triumph in a purchase. I can read a second-hand book catalogue with concentration that brings the smell of books into the room, the smoothness of old calfskin to my fingertips, the elegance of folio and quarto, black letter and morocco before my eyes. I can want a book with a passion close to crime, yet my thought is never of value that may increase, only of reading and possession.

It is only after many years of feeling my way that I have learned how strong and real a pleasure an amateur can find and how easily he can find it. In spite of my scattering interests, I did once believe with grandfather that one should never undertake anything without intending to become fully expert in it. For that reason I paid only casual attention to birds. I was a little afraid of their complexity, and far more afraid of the exact knowledge and subtle distinctions of the ornithologists I knew. I am still far from an ornithologist, but I am a wholehearted amateur of birds. I am not ashamed that I cannot instantly recognize all the subtle differences between species and subspecies, nor even visualize them clearly from the painstaking descriptions in the bird books. It has occurred to me that the greatest ornithologists have nearly always been artists; I think of Gould and Audubon, of Allan Brooks and Peter Scott and Roger Tory Peterson. Such men have a natural eye for color and form and light, refined by training, strengthened by use, that I can never hope to have. Yet my own eyes have now stored up many impressions of form and flight and movement, and I have even taught myself tricks of observation that let me apply what I have read in the books. I shall never be expert, never sure in difficult identifications, never fully wise in the probabilities of migration and distribution. But I am no longer afraid of birds or ashamed of my incompetence with them; I am free to learn about them to the best of my limited powers, to enjoy them, perhaps even to add some fraction to the sum of knowledge about them.

Perhaps I have stretched my argument too far, made too much of the virtues of being an amateur; the creative or interpretive writer is by definition an amateur of many things. But I think that men, especially men who live busy and intense professional lives, are too often afraid to be amateurs; the long-drawn complexity and intense specialization of their jobs makes them feel that they can never have time to learn anything else well enough to find pleasure and confidence in it. They believe with grandfather that one must be very good or keep away. There is real loss in this. Amateurs are the only driving force that can carry a civilization beyond a certain limited point of development. It seems to me that North American civilization is ready for a revival of amateurs in numbers and skills beyond those of any previous civilization. If so, it can grow something as wildly important as a new flowering of the human race.

COUNTRY LIVING

IT IS EASY TO BECOME SOFT AND lyrical about living in the country; still easier, to judge from some fairly recent and very successful books by lady writers, to become cute and quaint and funny as all get out. I don't know which of these choices is the better part, because I have lived nearly all my life in the country and have never felt either lyrical or cute about it. What I do feel is that living in the country is a whole lot more natural and normal than living in a city.

It may not be desirable at all to be natural or normal, even as approximately natural and normal as living in the country under modern conditions forces one to be. Apparently most North American people don't feel that it is, or they would not so persistently crowd closer and closer together on sixty-foot lots, in apartments piled one on top of the other or in buildings where one wall does the work of two. By so crowding themselves they do achieve in very large measure an objective that man has had from his earliest existence, which is freedom to pursue his work with a minimum of interference from the elements and other natural obstacles. It seems a completely logical development from the first thought of shelter, the first use of fire, the first barricade against wild animals. If these things were desirable, how much more so is the weatherproof warmth of a modern house, the intricate protections of a close community, the manifold services that can be reasonably cheap and efficient if the crowding is close enough. The world is too big and tough and dangerous for man. In his cities he can forget the realities of finding food, making shelter, creating warmth for himself, and protecting himself, in the single reality of making enough money to pay for all these things to be done for him.

The resulting freedom is an important thing, perhaps all-important. Man is free to go about his work and his pleasure for twenty-four hours of every day, with brief periods out for sleeping and eating. And if he lives in a city of respectable size, the wit and wisdom and all the high art of his time are close at hand and at his service, usually for a most moderate fee. He can exclaim with the late Dr. Johnson and other more recent and more derivative sages that "no man, at all intellectual," is willing to leave the city; though Johnson said also, "they who are content to live in the country are *fit* for the country," and seems himself to have developed a little shamefaced feeling for it occasionally in the Hebrides.

Things have changed a lot since Johnson's day and many of the differences between town and country have faded with improved communications, shortened distances, and a thousand modern inventions, from the automobile to the cheaply printed book and the phonograph record. But the crowding into the cities goes on and man in his enormous gregariousness seems to find it the answer to his problems. He has fitted chosen sections of the earth with floors of asphalt and concrete, has almost succeeded in drawing an all-protecting roof over them and flooding them with artificial light and warmth. Within this insulation, which he is steadily making more impervious to the intrusions of the normal world, he goes about his brisk business. He must still drag around with him the handicaps and pleasures of an earthly body, but perhaps that too can be adapted and refined into something more nearly fitted to his needs—a nylon stocking from a forest tree.

If this impressive emancipation makes for a heavy dependence upon the continuing effectiveness of machines and services, it should also provide enormous opportunities for human development and human happiness. The nature of happiness is a difficult and complicated thing. There is a theory, probably quite a sound one, that the finer, more brilliant shades of happiness are only perceptible to highly civilized people; true, this capacity is counterbalanced by a similar capacity for greater despair, more intense misery, but the sum of a man who has capacity for heights and depths should be greater than the sum of one whose range is limited. I wonder about this a good deal because the only people I have ever seen who impressed me as being absolutely happy are the Eskimos.

I may be wrong about Eskimos; I don't know them as well as I should to write about them. But I think of the Eskimos at a tiny settlement on the Arctic Ocean, coming in one by one as we sat at supper to lean against the wall and watch and smile. The first would gradually slide down into a squatting position, then the second beside him, and the third and the fourth. They would listen to us and nod their heads and smile; one would nudge another and say something and they all would laugh. They were happy.

I think of coming into a landing at a summer sealing camp, still farther north. Fifty or sixty Eskimos met us as we stepped ashore and each and every one of them shook hands with us, in laughter and happiness. Later, as we sat on the steps of the Hudson Bay factor's house, another fifty or more who had missed the landing came up and with these also we shook hands. Again I felt happiness, not just within myself, but from every man, woman, and child whose hand touched mine. It was a quiet happiness, but open and flowing in laughter and smiles that seemed to light a brilliant world.

I remember going out with a group of young Eskimos to collect the fish from set gill nets. Only one of them, my friend Peter, could speak English, but he translated back and forth for all of us and there seemed no gap in understanding. The catches were poor and the fish were enormously important— or would be in two or three short months when the world was ice and snow and darkness again—but we laughed over every fish and every lack of fish and were men together. I remember going up the Coppermine River with Peter and a simple French priest on a grim grey day of cold and mist. We shot at wolves on the high banks of the river, studied their tracks in the lower places; we made tea and warmed ourselves in the priest's tiny cabin near the falls; and again we were happy, without effort or thought, without restraint or effusion.

I think of the Eskimo girl who sewed bells to the hem of her *artiga* so that everyone would know when she got up in the night to go to her white lover. I think of the more tragic but equally revealing simplicity of two Eskimos who once murdered a policeman. Only a short while before two Eskimos of a nearby band had been sentenced to imprisonment for a murder that had some extenuating circumstances; they had served their term in the comparative comfort of the Mounted Police post, with food and clothing supplied by the beneficent government that had sentenced them. It seemed to the second murderers that death of a white man was easier purchase for two or three years of life in their formidable country than the effort of hunting and traveling and trapping.

I believe the Eskimo represents the summit of man's achievement in survival and adaptability. He lives in a barren, shelterless land of cold and wind-chill, without sun for almost half the year; he lives because he has skill and endurance in hunting, because he has learned that two caribou hides back to back, with the hair sides outward to cold and inward to body warmth, will protect him against cold; because he knows secrets of oil and blubber; because he understands the uses of snow against cold, because he has learned to breed and use dogs, because he has always made just enough effort to capture and store the yield of the arctic summer against the arctic winter. By any modern standards he lives under intolerable conditions. He has no security, even of life itself, for longer than six months at a time. He is never shielded, except by his own immediate, tenuous effort, from the most brutal realities of climate. Let the hunting fail, the seals be too distant, the caribou hard to find, the fish scarce, and he is faced with freezing and starvation. If a man is an inadequate hunter, it is reason enough for his wife to set him aside and take another husband. Women drop from hunting parties to give birth and catch up; if the trip be overhard and dangerous, pressed for time by weather or season or short rations, she must kill her child and hasten on her way; else both would die or the whole party be threatened. It is hard to imagine a life closer to the earth's bitterest realities. Yet these people survive and find a happiness so deep and sure and real, so clearly worthwhile, that no crusader from a superior civilization has yet dared tamper with it in any serious degree.

These are extremes, the insulated security of the city, the ironbound reality of the Western Arctic, and there is no argument to be drawn from them except that man can find happiness of body and mind and soul in both. Whether the simple quality of one happiness is worth more than the complex bittersweetness of the other I do not know. But it is difficult not to feel more of the calm reason for being that men seek in the life of the Eskimo than in the life of the city. If this is so it would seem that the city's civilization has overlooked something, perhaps that the realities of his world and a measure of freedom to face them are an essential part of man's happiness.

For my part I would not wish too much insulation for myself or my children. Since they are not born to it I would see them protected from the rigorous reality of the Eskimo's life, where the demands of survival are so pervasive that there is little room for growth. Yet I would protect them also from the abysmal ignorance of the city, from the naïveté of extreme sophistication. Better the country child's momentary fear of an elevator than the city child's belated discovery that milk comes from a cow; better a sureness with wind and rain and earth than native understanding of traffic lights and streetcars and department stores.

I should not write of these things as though they were mutually exclusive; even Johnson knew better than that. "It is easy," he wrote, "to set at home and conceive rocks and heath, and waterfalls . . . but it is true likewise, that these ideas are always incomplete, and that at least, till we have compared them with realities, we do not know them to be just. . . . Regions mountainous and wild, thinly inhabited, and little cultivated, make a great part of the earth, and he that has never seen them, must live unacquainted with much of the face of nature, and with one of the great scenes of human existence." So he sat, very self-conscious, reluctantly bucolic, looking out over the spareness of the Hebrides, and felt that he knew something of the great waste spaces of the earth. "Yet," he asked, "what are these hillocks to the ridges of Taurus, or these spots of wildness to the desarts of America?"

I think only that transition is easier the other way, from country to town. There is much to love and admire in cities. I once lived for nearly two years in London and was happy there and productive, though I had few concerns I could name outside my work. The city itself was endless interest and fascination. I walked through it at nights for enormous distances, watching and talking and feeling, though I was not equipped to understand as I should have. I began to know parts of it so well that I felt I had place and share in them. I came to know cab drivers and waiters and news vendors and barmen, even a few artists and actors and singers and writers who, like myself, were on the slippery borders of their respective professions. I loved it all, even felt at home in it. Yet it seemed in no way surprising or difficult to leave it all and come west again.

I have known and loved many cities since that time. I find cities exciting and heart-warming, full of life and often lonely, always gay and sad together, brilliant and dull, parasitic and creative. There is all the difference in the world between a city where one has close friends, however few, and a city where one is altogether strange. Yet a strange city is exciting, any city is exciting and exhilarating and inspiring in the first few hours after one has arrived there, and no one feels this more sharply than does the countryman. It is only later that he questions the excitement, wonders about the apparent hurry and purpose, listens more closely to its tone and finds it empty.

Perhaps, after all, fitness is everything and one is fittest for the life of one's choice, city or country. For there is choice, and it is choice, fundamentally, that has built the cities and turned people to live in them. I have made my choice long since and can never now go back from it. I might go to the city tomorrow and remain there in apartment and subway and office building until I die, but I should remain a countryman, with a countryman's values and insights, a countryman's blindness and simplicity. I want the seasons to have full meaning for me; I want to know storm and fine weather and to have to be out in both; I want a river within sight and sound of me, the sea and the hills within reach. I want the quiet, reluctant, yet faithful intimacy of country people. I want to go on learning one tree from another, one bird from another, good soil from bad, a sound hay crop from a poor one, healthy growth from unhealthy. I want to go on leaving my doors unlocked, my windows unlatched, my shades undrawn.

I want to continue as a man not too remote from the sensations and thoughts of my forebears. I want at least the illusion that I have a place and part in the natural world, some measure of power and freedom to supply my own needs, to protect my own and instruct my own. I want to go on believing it is worthwhile to search for purpose and plan and meaning in everything about me.

Perhaps all this is available within the insulation of a city. Perhaps more advanced truths are more readily available there and man's proper destiny is to free himself to their pursuit. Country-bred, I wonder if freedom from living may not be freedom from life itself. City people talk of "escape" when they talk of country living. To me a cow is reality. Escape is homogenized, pasteurized milk, delivered to the back door in a disposable carton.

FEBRUARY

Whenever it rained in Feb-
ruary grandfather would gaze out of the dining-room window and say, "February fill-dyke." He believed it, sometimes
acted on it, yet even in England I could never feel convinced
by the phrase; my short years of experience held against it,
whatever an older generation might have thought.

Here on Vancouver Island February is not a time of thaw
and wetness, though we do have February thaws when the
snow sags, flat white and rotten for a few days, until the frost
hardens it again or a new snow falls. These brief thaws are
themselves a relief and a symbol of the month. They start the
little streams running bank high with white or pale yellow
water, fresh and clean and lively over beds of sunken, saturated
snow. Other streamlets run steadily in many unexpected places,
draining hollows but seeming splendidly strong and permanent in their few days of life. In the hollows they drain, the
snow is a heavy translucent soup that stirs underfoot and
stops at once. In the woods it is deep and soft and sugary, and
the buds of willow and alder are healthy and strong, almost
bursting.

For the most part I think of February as clean, light frosts at night and bright sun by day. It is the sun that is the month's character, a sun of warmth and brilliance to lift everything from the dark and heavy slowness of the year's depths. All the months of the year have colors for me, as I suppose they have for most people. February's is a clear and even brown, a color of sunlight on fallen leaves and wet earth as they appear from under the snow. It grows out of the grey-white of January, the black and dark grey of December and November, and its nearest matching time must be midway between the straw color of September and the heavy brown of October. But February goes forward into the lighter brown of March, the pale, clear blue of April, the hawthorn white of May. It is a color of resurrection, holding in itself somehow June's blue-green, July's fire red, and the deep and solid blue of August. It is safe and right that leaf buds should swell a little in February and color flow into the willow switches, that bulbs should thrust under the snow and insects stir again.

February is not spring and no wise man wants it to be spring, because the effect of later frosts on tender things opened too soon can be so bitter and so lasting. But the earth does stir itself under the February sun and all creatures stir with it. There are scents on air that was coldly scentless in January, there is a renewal of color and light; even my own protected, insensitive body feels a new freedom of movement, a willingness to put forth effort for the sheer pleasure of effort; there is an appreciably longer day in which to do things, an easing of wind's intensity, cloud's shadow, and a slower kindness in the fall of evening.

Single robins come back in February, cowbirds return to the pastures as the snow leaves them, purple finches join the juncos and towhees and song sparrows around the house. Along the beaches migrating brant show again, riding the short breaking swells with sea gull's grace made lovelier by showy black and white of their powerful bodies. The ducks on the river are in fine plumage and mallard and goldeneyes already move in pairs. The merganser drakes parade in brilliant succession, sometimes as many as a dozen of them, in splashing and display before still unpersuaded females. Occasionally one comes closely upon a Barrow's goldeneye and can see the richly purple gloss of his head and swollen crest in the sunlight; but the mallard's head is of such multiple, tiny-feathered brilliance that the full strength of the sun strikes green fire from it, even in flight.

I remember all these things of February, but the month's most faithful sign, unaccountable, yet predictable as bird migration, sure as the lengthening days, welcome as the retreat of anchor ice from the river bottoms, is the children's rediscovery of skipping rope. I can hear them now, on the terrace outside the study window, shuffle of feet, flick of the rope on stone, and always the rhymes, brought from the Lord knows where, mutilated and adapted by the Lord knows how many generations of February children, but holding always the rhythms of jumping feet and challenging rope.

> *"On the mountain stands a lady.*
> *Who she is I do not know,*
> *All she wants is gold and silver,*
> *All she wants is a fine young man.*
> *So come in, my dearest Lin,*
> *While I go off to play."*

And out jumps that one while another takes her place. That particular rhyme seems timeless and without place. Its comment is routine; I like to think it reflects a fragment of parental gossip dropped with more or less harm in some New England village and carried westward by the covered wagons. But it may just as easily have crossed an ocean as well as plains and mountains. Another favorite, whose social comment smacks of the tenement and the big city, is handled here with little expression.

> *"I had a little Teddy Bear,*
> *His name was Tiny Tim,*
> *Put him in the bathtub,*
> *To see if he would swim.*
> *He drank all the water,*
> *He ate all the soap.*
> *In comes the doctor, in comes the nurse,*
> *In comes the lady with the big fat purse.*
> *Out goes the doctor, out goes the nurse,*
> *Out goes the lady with the big fat purse."*

I like the picture I get from it of pigtails bobbing, of sideways glances, of little red tongues thrust out as soon as the lady's broad back is safely bent to the entrance of car or carriage.

This next, touching experience more closely, is sung with expression but I am never quite sure whether the expression is faintly sardonic or casually respectful. Perhaps it varies and a more sensitive ear than mine would be able to tell which children are the cynics, which the loyalists.

> *"I am a Girl Guide, dressed in blue.*
> *These are the actions I must do:*
> *Stand at attention.*
> *Stand at ease.*
> *Bend my elbows, bend my knees,*
> *Salute to the captain, curtsy to the queen,*
> *And never turn my back on the Union Jack,*
> *Red, white and blue."*

February

I can't help feeling that our children may be underprivileged in their inheritance of rhymes. All those they know are in English, yet I should judge that less than half the children in their school are of English-speaking extraction. Are there no foreign-language rhymes? Or do they fade from memory in the gap between school days and emigration? And do the rhymes of the children of the Kentucky hills, of New York and Brooklyn and Montreal reach us here? Perhaps San Francisco inspired this one:

> "Teacher, Teacher have you heard?
> Pop's going to buy me a mockingbird.
> If the mockingbird don't sing,
> Pop's going to buy me a diamond ring.
> If the diamond ring don't shine,
> Pop's going to buy me a streetcar line.
> If the streetcar line don't run,
> Pop's going to buy me a shooting gun.
> If the gun don't shoot,
> Pop's going to buy me a bathing suit.
> If the bathing suit gets tore,
> Pop's going to buy me a candy store.
> If the candy store burns down,
> Pop and I are leaving town."

Probably not San Francisco; streetcars are hardly adequate identification and the line of northward travel seems faintly illogical. Yet last summer I compared notes with my friend Ed Adams, of Seattle, who is also a fan of what he calls jump-rope rhymes, and we found that our children are skipping or jumping to much the same words. Ed has preserved a few in a slim little volume printed at the Silver Quoin Press in Seattle. I have a secret resolve to listen again, some February twenty years from now, to my grandchildren marking the longer days and the snow's withdrawal. Unless she has been declared ideologically unsuitable by then, or perhaps even if she has, I shall expect to hear more of the lady with the big fat purse.

THE RIVER

I SHOULD LIKE TO HAVE MANY houses beside many rivers, except that a man can only live in one house at a time. If he had many houses by many rivers he would always be regretting the houses left empty and the rivers unwatched.

Perhaps I have had my share of waking and sleeping beside different rivers. Grandfather's house stood on the banks of one clear running little Dorset stream and another larger stream was only two or three hundred yards away across the fields. For years I lived in logging camps, most of them overlooking lakes or streams, or else made my own camp nightly beside whatever stream was nearest. Through part of two winters I ran trap lines from a cabin set in the fork of a river that drained a timbered valley. Even in London I managed to rent one room within sight of Thames, and another as near, though turned from it.

Now Ann and I have lived sixteen years within sight and sound of the Elk and seem likely to live here another sixteen or sixty years. It should be enough. Yet not so long ago I bid on a four-hundred-acre island lying in the mouth of a northern river; the island was listed in a tax sale and my bid didn't take it because the owner reclaimed, but my intention was definite enough. From time to time Ann and I idly explore the next large river valley north of us, searching always for

some place above flood level that commands a good stretch
of the river, upstream and down. And well south of here,
along the highway to Victoria, one comes suddenly upon a
tiny white church built among great maple trees at the entrance to a narrow bridge on a sharp curve. On the far side
of the bridge is a red-roofed frame house set well down on a
flat between the river and an old grass-grown bed that is dry
except in floodtime. The little river is slow and clear and deep
near the house, with an easy sloping bank on which there is
nearly always an upturned canoe or rowboat. Upstream, at a
bend, there is the half-hidden stir of a little rapid. I never pass
that house without wanting to live there for a spell. Yet I
know the river can flood and I suspect the house is set too well
down, too comfortably beside the river's workaday level to be
safe in flood.

I cannot altogether separate this obsession with rivers from
the lore and habit of fishing and hunting, yet I think it is a
natural thing for a man to love a river, and I think I should
still want to live by one if I had never caught a fish or fired a
gun. A river is life and light, especially in timbered country;
it is always the easiest natural way of travel and it is used as
such by many creatures besides man. No clean river can be
other than beautiful and it has changing beauty. Even a
streamlet can become impressive in floodtime and the greatest
of rivers has a light, almost intimate quality of gentleness at its
lowest summer level.

The Elk is not a big river. It flows at an average of twenty-
three hundred cubic feet a second throughout the year, at
thirty thousand cubic feet in extreme freshet, and about four
hundred cubic feet in its quietest moments. This last figure
works out at about a hundred and fifty thousand gallons a
minute, while the extreme freshet figure means something over
eleven million gallons a minute; even in gallons and minutes

the figures don't mean as much as they should, but here at the house that freshet figure is an awe-inspiring quantity of water going by very, very fast, so fast that every rock on the bottom throws a pattern on the surface and the bigger rocks break white water even when they are five or six feet under. The summer figure is a rippling flow so easy and gentle that I can pole the big canoe quite easily against the very center of the steep little rapid just above the house.

The Elk follows a pattern fairly common in the short mountainous streams of the coast. At its mouth there was once a flat tidal meadow, less than a mile square, shielded by a long sandspit and beloved by ducks and geese and swans. A big logging company's booming ground has long since chased the geese and most of the ducks away, dredging and pile-driving have changed the channels and hidden the meadow, but it is still a lovely place, made alive by the tidal changes and the many creatures that tolerate human activity and settlement. Ospreys hunt there and herons wait. Kildeer and yellowlegs and many sandpipers are there in spring; meadowlarks sing from the fence posts, grebes and mergansers nest in the slough, loons fish in the channel, mink and coon hunt the shorelines, an occasional bear comes down through the farms, cormorants perch on the piles, Bonaparte's gulls flock in to rest on the log booms.

Only a mile or two above tidewater the river is enclosed in a high, narrow canyon of rock, which it enters through a lovely fall of well over a hundred feet. The fall has always controlled the river's character, changing it sharply from a coastal stream with runs of salmon and all the other anadromous fish to a landlocked watershed; limiting its usefulness to canoe travelers and turning them away to trails and roads. And now at last it has meant power, the first dam above the falls, the big dam just below the first lake, the powerhouse at the foot of the canyon.

The first two big lakes take the river's name, Upper and Lower Elk Lake, but above the upper lake the river loses its own name in the name of the third and largest lake of its chain and becomes Strathcona River. This is always happening to rivers, sometimes without any logical break such as a lake to make it happen, and it serves a useful purpose in closely identifying the different reaches. But merely changing a name cannot make a river tributary to itself; it has always a true headwater, an ultimate source in spring or snowbank or glacier, whence it comes to gather its tributaries into its single purposeful bed that follows always the lowest floor of its valley to the sea. Our river rises in summer snow on the slopes of the high mountains to the south of Strathcona Lake, gathers the tiny streams from other slopes and peaks until it is a sizable creek, joins another creek almost as large as itself, and comes coldly and quietly into the big lake through a tangled flat where elk and beaver work.

For twenty miles from there the lake is the river's bed and along both sides of the lake are high mountains, five and six and seven thousand feet high, cut by short deep valleys that bring more water from snow fields and little lakes. In the length of the lake the river takes to itself seven major tributaries, each one from a valley of untouched timber, and a hundred lesser streams; as it leaves the lake it is full river size, broad and fine, and it takes another valley's river to itself just before it enters the upper lake.

I call the river mine, without owning any foot of it from source to sea and without any thought of possession in the ordinary sense. At one time or another I have walked most of the valley's length; I have traveled a good part of it by boat and canoe; I have waded most places where wading is possible and the fishing makes it worthwhile. I have blazed trees at the level of highest flood and have studied the depressions and hidden rocks of the bottom in lowest summer water. I know the rhythms of the salmon and trout runs of the length below the falls and something of the landlocked fish above the falls. I know where to expect beaver and elk and deer and bear and cougar. I know what ducks I shall see in summertime, where the geese and swans will find open water in freeze-up. I can name at least some of the May flies and stone flies and sedges that live out their lives along the river. I know the trees of its valley and some of the rock formations; I know the temperature of the mountain streams that feed it and the variations of temperature in the river itself when it has passed through the lakes. I can remember other years and recognize changes and make pronouncements that sound wise even to myself. In all this there is an intimacy akin to possession and far more important than possession. I do not want possession, only freedom of the river; and with every growth of knowledge and experience freedom grows.

Because I have learned so much of the river through fishing and watching fish, it is difficult to write of it without thinking of fish. From a fisherman's point of view almost everything about a river is related to fish and fishing. Floods or drought may mean disaster to spawning and hatch, or merely disappointed hopes of good fishing; birds and animals that live along the banks are predators or controls or both; insect life, in the water and out of it, is feed; lime content, temperature, weed growth, log jams, shallows or deeps, all have meaning in terms of fish and fishing. Even trees and brush overhanging the banks, even the work of beavers and muskrats, has bearing. It may seem a narrow view, but the interrelationships are so far reaching and complicated that it is really comprehensive; if anything is not included, the fisherman is almost certain to include it because observation is one of the keenest pleasures of his sport. A deer seen by the waterside, a yellowthroat's nest at the edge of a lake, the burst of dogwood blossoms along the banks in springtime, the curve of sunlit water over a smooth rock, all these things are important to his sport as the fish themselves, and he does not pass them by.

But for the accident of the falls, the Elk would be an even finer salmon river than it is; the streams above the lakes would have supported the spawning of thousands upon thousands of sockeye salmon and the lakes themselves would have raised the young fish through the year or two they spend in freshwater before migration. As it is, the Elk itself has only a mile or two of good spawning water and only one important tributary that the salmon can reach. In spite of this the river supports one of the most famous runs of big spring salmon in the world, as well as significant runs of two other salmon and two species of trout. The cycle of these runs, spawning, hatching of fry, growth of young fish, migration, and return, make much of the character of the lower river. It is on these, in the last analysis, that eagles and mergansers, ospreys and mallards and goldeneye, coon and mink and bear and otter depend, as does an important part of Elkhorn's population.

And the runs themselves, although the river is closed off above the falls, depend not only on this short two miles of breeding water, but upon the river's whole system. The stored snow under the virgin timber in the headwaters is the first resource; cut away the timber and much of it would be wasted, run off in times when the lower river did not need it. The delaying storage of the lakes is important, as is their power to settle silt of flood, to mingle temperatures and hold them low in storage; for silt chokes spawning beds, and high temperatures speed hatching times, low temperatures delay them too long. The aeration of all the rapids and falls above the lakes, perhaps that of the big falls themselves, is important to the fish and all life that feeds them. These things add up to the real river, a good strong flow of clear, clean water over a broad and rocky bed, rarely too strong, rarely too feeble, rarely too warm or too cold. They add up also, especially the lakes and the protecting timber of the hills, to the river's hundred and fifty thousand horsepower of electricity. And they are the country's beauty. It will be a foolish and criminal hand that interferes farther with them.

Because the dam is built above the falls and because it was built with reasonable care, it has not affected the salmon runs. In time, as new storage limits the river's extremes of high and low water, it may even improve them. If the summer's low of four hundred cubic feet a second is raised to fifteen hundred or more there will be better spawning room for more salmon. If the peak of the floods is lessened there will be no scouring of spawning beds. So long as the turbines are turning through the spells of cold weather, the water they discharge will keep the frost away from the eggs buried in the gravel.

The children and I look forward to the river's new summer flow. In June of a normal year water is breaking over the crest of the wing dam and there is good swimming behind it. By July we must take the canoe and cross to the big rock on the far side to find any depth of water. In August of a dry year even this is no good; we must pole our way upstream to the next big pool and there is not always time for that. Besides, we don't really like the big pool. With the river at a good height it is far more interesting to swim the rapid, coming down fast with the current, swinging in behind the big rock and working up along the shore to do it all again. As nearly as I can judge, fifteen hundred cubic feet a second should be just about perfect for this. There are some by-products to a fifteen-million-dollar dam that even the engineers don't know about.

If one had to live out a life whose sight was limited to the breadth of the river at one place, the full measure of the year and all the seasons would be in it, as plainly there as in the pages of the handsomest calendar ever drawn. It would be a record of contrasts and mergence: the slow moving black water of January's binding cold against the sunlit rush of melting snow in the heat of June; revealing shallowness of August, with brown and green algae on the rocks, wiped utterly away in November's bank-high torrent; March rains building the flow in murky haste, to settle into the cleaner, still growing run-off of April and May; September's hesitancy, broken by the spawning salmon, becoming October of the drowned and drifting leaves and the dying fish. One could watch and call the winter's weight and spring's delay from hold of fullness in July, look out and know how November winds had blown from the river's height in early December.

We live with the river and seldom forget it for long, but we are not always sharply conscious of it. The stranger hears its sound as he lies in bed waiting for sleep; we do not, unless we listen for it. For days on end we may scarcely think of the river, letting its weight and volume leap and slide away "unheeded as a threshold brook" in patterned flow towards the bridge and sea. This could be ungrateful failure, but I consider it rather a secure familiarity that takes much for granted between whiles. Except for the river we should not be here, living and growing as a family on this particular soil. Without the river there would be no sense in the way the windows look out from the house, the way the lawn runs and the trees are planted. Most of our days would be in some way different. And four different children than these would go out into the world, with different measures for their years.